POSTERS OF THE WPA

Christopher DeNoon

"The Federal Art Project of the Works Progress Administration is a practical relief project, which also emphasizes the best tradition of the democratic spirit. The WPA artist, in rendering his own impression of things, speaks also for the spirit of his fellow countrymen everywhere. I think the WPA artist exemplifies with great force the essential place which the arts have in a democratic society such as ours."

Franklin Delano Roosevelt
—Excerpts from the address delivered on the
occasion of the tenth anniversary of the opening
of the Museum of Modern Art, May 11, 1939.

POSTERS OF THE WPA

Christopher DeNoon

Introduction
Francis V. O'Connor, Ph.D.

A Remembrance of the WPA
Anthony Velonis

A Design Perspective
Jim Heimann

A Remembrance of the Federal Art Project
Richard Floethe

T h e   W h e a t l e y   P r e s s ■ P u b l i s h e r s ■ L o s   A n g e l e s
In Association with the University of Washington Press, Seattle

■

Published by The Wheatley Press, 3518 Cahuenga Boulevard West, Suite 205, Los Angeles, California 90068

Distributed by the University of Washington Press, P.O. Box 50096, Seattle, Washington 98145

ISBN 0-295-96543-6
Library of Congress Catalog Card Number 87-50519

The publisher wishes to acknowledge and thank Henry Vizcarra, whose resolve, spirit, and taste carried this project to successful completion.

Edited by Letitia O'Connor and Diana Rico
Designed by 90 Degrees, Los Angeles
Art direction by Henry Vizcarra
Typeface Kabel, designed in 1928 by Rudolf Koch, who was born in Nuremberg, in 1876 and worked as a book designer
Typeset by Scarlet Letters, Los Angeles
Printed on 86 lb. U-light matte coated paper
Printed in Japan by Dai Nippon Printing Company

Dimensions are in inches and centimeters; height precedes width. All posters are silkscreens unless otherwise indicated. Numbers in brackets refer to figure numbers.

Front cover	Back cover	Frontispiece
Jack Rivolta	Artist unknown	Vera Bock
New York, NY	Chicago, IL	New York, NY
71 x 56 cm.	76 x 51 cm.	71 x 56 cm.
28 x 22 in.	30 x 20 in.	28 x 22 in.

Dedication: for Susan and Nevis

ACKNOWLEDGEMENTS

The author wishes to take this opportunity to thank some of the many people who contributed their time and talents to this book:
Jim Heimann for his continuous support and unfailing belief that "It's gonna happen"; Roleen Heimann Young for her infinite kindnesses; Nancy Gimbrone for the spark of an idea about the worth of W.P.A. Art; Henry Vizcarra for his design skills, professionalism and friendship; Freda Wheatley Vizcarra for her enthusiasm, her desire to see the posters in print and her attention to detail; Catherine Boyer for her years of encouragement and belief; Jerry Roth for supplying first hand information about the New York City Poster Project; Tony and Betty Velonis for sharing their memories and their home; Francis V. O'Connor for his thoughtful words of introduction and for his pioneering research into the works of the Federal Art Project; Letitia Burns O'Connor for the (relatively) painless application of her well honed skills as editor to a rather lumpy manuscript; Diana Rico for polishing away the rough edges and for making the words work; The Library of Congress for its myriad wonders and eager staff especially, Elena Millie for providing access to the Poster Collection she curates, Jerry Kerns for speeding orders along, and Reid S. Baker for the hundreds of first rate transparencies he shot; The New York Public Library and its staff particularly Robert Rainwater and Roberta Waddell for their willingness to share the resources of "Researchers Heaven"; Richard Floethe for providing all the answers to many questions; Dr. Lorraine Brown, Associate Director, and Ruth Kern of the Institute on the Federal Theatre Project and New Deal Culture at George Mason University for all their help in easing the problems of long distance research; Krys Cianciarullo for his always excellent photographs (and his reasonable rate too); Kenneth Cobb of the New York City Municipal Archives for the freedom to delve into that city's New Deal history; Robert Sindelir Director of Galleries and Visual Arts Programs at Miami-Dade Community College, Wolfson Campus for access to materials in the Mitchell Wolfson Jr. Collection of Decorative and Propaganda Arts; Vikki Boyer for providing a base of operations when working in D.C.; David Peck for the unintimidating academic atmosphere that encouraged the search; Cynthia Ott of the Archives of American Art for her assistance and good humor; Steve Skinner for his laser expertise and for the one hundred favors I hope I can repay; Eunice Halls for providing information and photographs of her husband Richard Halls; Louis B. Siegriest for providing access to the "missing poster"; Arthur Silberman of the Native American Painting Reference Library for his generous loan of materials; Tammy Taniguchi for her professional skills and enthusiasm; Mary Ryan for her gallery and her interest; Christopher Korody for the loan of appropriate technology. And to my parents Roberta Ives DeNoon and John DeNoon for instilling in me the love of books.

Contents

■

Introduction by Francis V. O'Connor, Ph.D.   **7**

Posters of the WPA   **13**

The New Deal and the Visual Arts   **13**

The Birth of the Poster Divisions   **17**

A New Golden Age   **23**

The Decline of the Federal Art Project   **26**

The Fate of the WPA Posters   **32**

Federal Art Project Posters   **37**

Federal Theatre Project Posters   **57**

A Remembrance of the WPA by Anthony Velonis   **72**

U.S. Travel Bureau Posters   **81**

Education and Civic Activity Posters   **87**

A Design Perspective by Jim Heimann   **108**

Health and Safety Posters   **113**

A Remembrance of the Federal Art Project by Richard Floethe   **128**

Federal Music Project and Federal Dance Project Posters   **133**

Federal Writers Project Posters   **139**

World War II Posters   **143**

Portfolio   **153**

Selected Bibliography   **172**

Reproduction Credits   **173**

Index   **174**

1
Artist unknown
New York, NY
71 x 56 cm.
28 x 22 in.

Introduction
WPA Posters: Murals in Miniature
by Francis V. O'Connor, Ph.D.

The WPA Federal Art Project is most often remembered for its murals—the ultimate manifestation of what would be called today "public art." Its painted walls in schools, hospitals, airports, and other public buildings, along with the murals commissioned by the Treasury Department's Section of Painting and Sculpture in our nation's post offices and court houses, constitute a stylistically variegated heritage of nearly 4,000 permanent, pictorial environments, the great majority of which have survived to take their place in the history of our visual culture.

At the opposite pole from New Deal murals were its posters—also meant to be seen democratically from public walls—but doomed by their topicality to survive by accident, if at all. As the author points out in this pioneering study of New Deal posters, only about 2,000 examples from 35,000 designs survive, though about 2,000,000 copies were printed during eight years. This is the inevitable fate of posters, of course, but it was also caused by that cultural myopia which always seems to distance the present image. It took nearly thirty years and another generation to begin to see New Deal iconography, so brilliantly set forth in WPA posters, as important.

I was involved in that regeneration of perception, and one of my most vivid recollections concerns the discovery of the country's largest cache of WPA posters in the Library of Congress. Late in 1965 I learned that the University of Maryland, whose faculty I had just joined, owned a large collection of objects from the government projects of the 1930s. These had been rescued from destruction in a government warehouse by several former New Deal artists in the department, including Mitchell Jameson and Herman Maril. I proposed to do an exhibition of this material, and the idea was accepted. The University's collection consisted mostly of mural studies, and I proceeded to fill in easel works, prints, sculpture—and posters—from other sources, to create a comprehensive survey of all the art forms

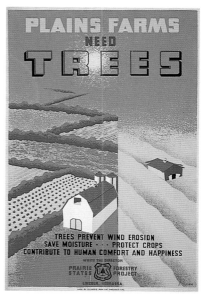

2
Joseph Dusek
Chicago, IL
76 x 51 cm.
30 x 20 in.

■

sponsored by the New Deal projects.

A little digging in the National Archives revealed that a large quantity of WPA posters had been allocated to the Library of Congress, and I called the chief of the prints and photographs division, Dr. Alan Fern (now director of the Smithsonian's National Portrait Gallery), to see if some of those posters might be lent to my show. At first they could not be located. But on the morning of February 15, 1966 I met with Dr. Fern and discovered that a record of the allocation had been found indicating that the posters were stored in one of the vast library's corner towers. A large key was produced, and we adventured a long climb up a very dusty, cobweb-festooned, spiral staircase until we came to a heavy door. Unlocked, this creaked open to reveal sinister sights and sounds: a large, musty, circular room at the very top of the building, stuffed with saw-horse tables heaped with ancient circus posters and filled with a crackling cacaphony of clicks that echoed about the domed chamber. Investigation revealed this to be the Library's pigeon control center, and the raucous noise generated by electrical wall units which charged wires set along the innumerable ledges and ornamental crevices of the grand old Beaux Arts building, the better to give hot foots to any winged being who might roost thereon!

Amid the heaps of circus posters and pigeon goosers we eventually came upon a large wooden case with a WPA shipping label which, after we had blackened our hands prying it open, was found to contain a wide-ranging national selection of WPA posters in pristine condition. Of all the art and documentation from this period I have discovered dirtying my hands in unlikely places, this find was the most unforgettable, given the bizarre context and the wealth uncovered. Ultimately I selected a number of posters, and used those from the various divisions of the WPA Federal Art Project to introduce the relevant sections of my exhibition. Later the Library, like so many other institutions that discovered their New Deal treasures in the late 1960s, accessioned the posters, and a number of the best are reproduced in this visually exciting book.

Three things make these posters significant and effective.

First, they represent the best of that impulse of the era in general, and the WPA Federal Art Project in particular, to integrate the fine and the practical arts. The idea goes back at least to the English Pre-Raphaelites of the mid-nineteenth century, and was certainly reborn to modernism in the German Bauhaus of the 1920s. It is not surprising that a key leader of the WPA Poster Division, Richard Floethe (whose memoir appears elsewhere in this book), was trained there. These posters reflect the "synthetic cubism" of the School of Paris, the geometric abstraction of Kandinsky and the de Stijl, and the efforts of Stuart Davis and American abstract artists—particularly those in New York—to make aesthetically revolutionary design principles the basis of a socially revolutionary art.

Second, these posters display a visual vocabulary that speaks as directly and forcefully as words in getting simple, imperative messages across to the people. In this they echo the devices of muralists, especially in respect to scale. Though physically small—most are about 22 × 14 inches—these posters project an aura of monumentality that is a function of their flat, screen-printed colors, and four elegant compositional devices employed alone or in combination: centricity, axial symmetry, diagonals, and overlapping. All of these formal elements engage the eye, emphasize the legibility of the motif and its message, and involve the viewer's sensory experience in the spatial dynamics of each visual unit. Like good murals, they relate in micro to architectural conventions dependent on human size to justify scale relationships. This illusion of a spatial environment with which the viewer can identify despite abstract innovations is the secret of their impact—and their

■

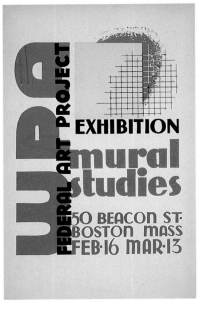

3
Artist unknown
Boston, MA
56 x 36 cm.
22 x 14 in.

promise of a future that was not to be.

Third, these posters anticipate what might have been artistically, had the New Deal's cultural programs not been terminated by World War II. It is clear that no "WPA style" had been formulated when the project began in 1935. But one was certainly emerging toward the end of the decade both on the Federal Art Project and in some of the more advanced Treasury murals. The WPA and Treasury walls of Ben Shahn, Seymour Fogel, Anton Refregier, Philip Guston, and James Brooks, all attest to a vital, modernist aesthetic sensibility slowly coalescing in the 1940s, influenced by the liberating experience of mural painting at the New York World's Fair. That sensibility was, however, most fully developed and disseminated in the poster division, where the small size of the works and the immediacy of deadlines provided an impetus to creative daring that the more cumbersome procedures of mural patronage and painting tended to inhibit.

What might have been can only be glimpsed and conjectured, but this book's revelation of WPA posters provides a hint of what WPA murals could have achieved had there been the time, the imagination, the freedom, and the bureaucratic courage to continue the projects well into the 1940s. But that was not to be, and now we can only speculate how American art would have developed if the artistic energies that these miniature surrogate walls reveal had been allowed to develop parallel to the other powerful visions nurtured during the WPA era.

Francis V. O'Connor is an independent historian of American art who holds a doctorate from The Johns Hopkins University. He has written extensively about the New Deal projects of the 1930s and the Abstract Expressionist period that followed. His most recent publications include a catalogue raisonné of Jackson Pollock's oeuvre, essays on the murals of Diego Rivera, and a series of articles on the psychodynamics of creativity.

4
Artist unknown
Chicago, IL
71 x 56 cm.
28 x 22 in.

5
In January, 1932 10,000 unemployed marched from Pittsburgh to Washington, D.C. Indicative of the government's laissez-faire attitude toward social problems was President Hoover's response that he could offer no assurances of work or federal aid.

Posters of the WPA

O ne of the most fascinating and vital developments of American graphic design
took place between 1935 and 1943, years
darkened by the Great Depression and World
War II. In this remarkable eight-year period,
the Works Progress Administration (WPA) printed two million posters
from thirty-five thousand designs. It was an innovative time, charac-
terized by experimentation, fresh ideas, and avant-garde thinking; the
result was, as noted at the time by **P.M. Weekly**, "poster art more vital
than any this country has ever known." And yet in the years that followed, little attention was given to this extraordinary design activity. The
story of the WPA posters and the artists who designed them is one of
the most interesting and unjustly overlooked chapters in the history of
American art.

The New Deal and the Visual Arts

Unemployment in the United States reached an all-time high during the
Great Depression. Nearly 30 percent of our nation's able work force had
no jobs to go to in the morning, no paychecks to bring home at the end
of the week. But in the early 1930s, in response to this debilitating crisis,
an act unprecedented in U.S. history occurred: Franklin D. Roosevelt's
New Deal Administration instituted work relief programs to create jobs
for citizens who had been displaced from employment in every sector
of the economy—not only technicians and mechanics, but scholars,
artists, and craftspersons as well. Visual artists, never traditionally viewed
as a necessary part of the American work force, especially welcomed
this opportunity to practice their crafts.

As is not unusual with government agencies, it took a few
years—and several changes in title and function—to iron out the details

6
Jack Rivolta
New York, NY
28 x 54 cm.
11 x 21¼ in.

of this new bureaucratic structure. Roosevelt's work relief program began in 1933 and was called, variously, the Temporary Emergency Relief Administration (TERA), the Public Works of Art Project (PWAP), and the Civilian Works Administration (CWA). In July 1935, the program finally stabilized as Federal Project Number One, a section of the Works Progress Administration's Division of Professional Service Projects. "Federal One" administered four projects: the Federal Theatre Project, the Federal Music Project, the Federal Writers Project, and the Federal Art Project.

The Federal Art Project (FAP) quickly became the main employer of the nation's artists. By 1938 the FAP existed in all 48 states and was making it possible for artists to "continue to literally stay alive and paint," as abstract painter Lee Krasner has said. Krasner, who considered the WPA program a "lifesaver," would go on to achieve great prominence in the art world, as would a long list of others nurtured by

7
Stacks of posters in the crowded storage area for New York City poster unit indicate the prolific output of the project.

8
Foster Humfreville
and Alex Kallenberg
New York, NY
71 x 56 cm.
28 x 22 in.

the FAP, including Will Barnet, Stuart Davis, Alice Neel, Louise Nevelson, Jackson Pollock, and Willem de Kooning. Forty-one percent of the WPA artists nationwide were women.

Its budgets comprised only about one percent of the WPA's total expenditure, but the FAP's output was as significant as the dams, roads, public housing, hospitals, job training, and educational services provided by other branches of the WPA. Today the best known works generated by the WPA art programs are probably the ubiquitous government-sponsored Post Office murals, although murals in public buildings were the function, not of the FAP, but of the Treasury Relief Art Project, or TRAP. What's less well remembered but equally important is that vast numbers of easel paintings, woodcuts, lithographs, photographs, watercolors, sculptures, and other art forms were produced, and American folk designs were preserved as well, all under the auspices of the FAP. "We were doing what we most wanted to do and getting paid a living wage to do it," recalls mural painter Edward Laning. "Oh, it was a glorious time."

The FAP's activities didn't stop with providing employment for artists, either. At a time when most Americans had had little or no exposure to art—venues for art exhibitions, for example, existed only in major urban centers—the FAP maintained more than a hundred Community Art Centers around the country. In cities as far-flung as Raleigh, North Carolina; Price, Utah; Melrose, New Mexico; and Sioux City, Iowa; FAP art centers regularly held exhibitions and offered art classes to the public [56, 70–72].

The art centers grew out of the democratic philosophy that the spiritual and aesthetic pleasures of art, rather than being reserved for an educated elite, should be available to the widest possible numbers of people. And it was from this same philosophy that

9
Artists dramatized the need for jobs in this 1934 demonstration in New York's Union Square, one year before the establishment of the Federal Art Project. One placard refers to the destruction of Diego Rivera's mural in Rockefeller Center.

the WPA / FAP Poster Divisions—today little known, but in the 1930s a vital and important sector of the WPA—emerged.

The Birth of the Poster Divisions

During the Depression as many as one-third of the artists involved nationally with the WPA / FAP worked in New York City, traditionally regarded as the art center of the United States. Thus, it's not surprising to learn that the WPA / FAP poster divisions were born there. But another reason was the city's feisty mayor, Fiorello La Guardia, and a couple of his pet projects of the day.

La Guardia had launched an anti-slot machine campaign. Photographs and newsreels of the period show the mayor gleefully axing confiscated slot machines and pulling levers on barges to dump dozens more into the Hudson River. He had also begun to promote a regular "Fish Tuesday" in an effort to stimulate a depressed fishing industry. To publicize these campaigns, the city's administrators created the Mayor's Poster Project in conjunction with the federal CWA in February 1934. The posters—individually produced, handpainted one-of-a-kinds—proved quite effective in getting the mayor's messages across.

When the New York City poster-production department was completely absorbed by the federal government in 1935, the first WPA / FAP poster division was born. Initially, the poster divisions were nothing more than tiny groups of poster painters turning out very limited volumes of work. Each poster was lettered and painted by hand, a painstakingly slow process that is highlighted in a photograph from the early years of the Chicago Poster Division: 20 or so artists, some in smocks and eyeshades, sit facing two master posters propped up in the center of the small room. Before them on drafting tables are in-progress copies of the master posters, so big they cover entire desktops.

The combination of small staff and correspondingly small

10
The most recognized graphic symbol of the New Deal, the National Recovery Act's blue eagle, is shown here with its designer Charles T. Coiner.

■

output severely limited the scope of the poster program, a fact that was immediately noticed by an artist named Anthony Velonis when he joined the CWA poster project in 1934, before it had been absorbed by the WPA / FAP. A graduate of the New York University School of Fine Arts, Velonis had worked at Stern Brothers department store producing show cards for window displays and countertops. This experience and a later job making wallpaper had introduced him to a standard commercial art process, silkscreening, which he felt could be adapted to the government-sponsored posters.

Reputedly developed by Chinese artists some 2,000 years ago, silkscreening is a printing process in which a gauze screen of silk or other fabric, held taut in a frame, is painted with a blockout material or covered with a sheet of lacquer film cut as a stencil. Paint or ink is squeegeed through the screen onto the desired surface, and an image is created via the blocked-out portions, which the paint can't penetrate.

In the early years of the twentieth century, silkscreening was used primarily to produce short-run commercial items—point-of-purchase displays, banners, souvenir pennants and such—quickly and economically. Knowing this technique would increase the productivity of the poster division, Velonis obtained the approval of the division's administrator, John Weaver, to implement it and, with the help of other staff members, constructed frames and drying racks [129]. Once designs were completed and approved, Velonis and the other artists began producing their screens in a little workshop on one of the upper floors of the General Electric Building at 51st Street and Lexington Avenue.

The New York City poster division's earliest silkscreened posters were one- or two- color, but as familiarity with the process grew, complicated posters of up to eight colors were printed. The technique was so rapid that even with runs of six to eight colors, as many as 600 posters could be produced daily. The manufacturing itself became a collaborative, creatively stimulating process, with the artists designing the posters, deciding on colors, and hand-cutting the lacquer films with images and type, the printers screening the posters and placing them in racks to dry, and both parties sharing their technical expertise and trading opinions in order to obtain the best possible results.

So successful did the division become with this new method that it soon moved to larger facilities—first to 39th Street, then to 42nd Street, and finally to 110 King Street [7] in New York's commercial district, where the NYC/FAP workshops and administrative offices were headquartered. The staff, which at its height numbered about 35 designers, 20 printers, and 10 to 12 cutters who did nothing but cut lacquer film, received salaries ranging from $21 to $27 per week—enough to live decently, if not luxuriously, in mid-Depression Manhattan.

It wasn't just the new production method that enabled the New York City poster division to prosper; it prospered because it was filling a community need, a need shared by other communities who were establishing their own WPA/FAP poster divisions. Essentially, the services of the WPA/FAP poster artists were available to any government agency that wanted to make use of them. Posters were recognized not only as a powerful tool of communication but as a way of enriching American citizens' lives: "The poster provides the same service as the newspaper, the radio, and the movies, and is as powerful an organ of information, at the same time providing an enjoyable visual experience," wrote Ralph Graham, head of the Chicago poster division. Posters were a democratic, demystified form of art, available to and able to be appreciated by all.

An ever-growing demand for posters led FAP art teachers and other WPA/FAP poster divisions to query the New York City division about its successful new printing process. Since there was so little written information available, Velonis wrote a pamphlet titled **Technical**

11
An artist at work on a rough sketch.

12
Developed from a rough sketch, this example of a comprehensive layout or "tight tissue" is the final step before a poster goes into production.

13
Poster printers examine the screen and register the poster board before printing a second color. The work depicts one variation of the FAP logo also seen in figures 42–46.

14
Designed and written by Anthony Velonis, this 1937 pamphlet is the first work to explore silkscreening as a fine art process.

Problems of the Artist: Technique of the Silk Screen Process [14]. Published by the WPA, Velonis's work is the first to treat silkscreening as more than a commercial art process: "Printing media must come to be regarded in exactly the same way as the painter esteems his canvas, paints, and brushes. The finished work must convey the feeling that the artist has a certain amount of intimacy with his printing medium, no matter how mechanical," he stressed. Mindful of silkscreen's expressive and aesthetic potential, Velonis believed that the importance of the silkscreen process went far beyond its utility for printing large numbers of posters. As he predicted in 1937, "The silk-screen process…will undoubtedly play an important role in the future of fine arts."

Velonis did much to make that prediction come true. During his FAP tenure, he experimented with materials and techniques to extend the range of effects available to the silkscreen artist; he pushed to establish an experimental silkscreen unit in the Graphic

15
Shown here are drying racks used to store posters between color passes.

Art Division so that silkscreen prints were made alongside of etchings, aquatints, stone lithographs, and woodblocks; he helped convince the FAP to approve inclusion of silkscreens in WPA-sponsored art classes and FAP exhibitions nationwide; and in 1940 he collaborated with Carl Zigrosser, director at the Weyhe Gallery [16], to coin a new term— serigraph, from the Latin "seri" (silk) and the Greek "graphein" (to write or draw)—to distinguish the new, fine art use of silkscreening from the traditional, commercial art process. It is largely because of Velonis's pioneering efforts that silkscreening would attain a firm place among fine art printmaking methods used by WPA artists including Hyman Warsager, Bernard Schardt, Eugene Morley, Elizabeth Olds, Harry Gottlieb [28], Ruth Chaney [22], and Louis Lozowick and eventually employed by such artists as Josef Albers, Alexander Calder, Stuart Davis, Robert Motherwell, Robert Rauschenberg, Frank Stella, and Andy Warhol.

Velonis's silkscreen-information pamphlet was widely

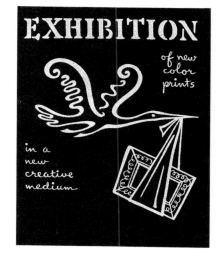

16
Although the word does not appear on the catalogue cover, this exhibition at the Weyhe Gallery, NY, introduced serigraphy, "a new creative medium," to the art historical lexicon.

17
A greeting card designed by the Chicago
FAP poster unit.

distributed to WPA art centers across the nation when it was published. As one of the main sources of technical information for the silkscreen poster units, the pamphlet directly contributed to the growth of the units. They also boomed because the process was not only simple and practical but inexpensive as well: records for 1937 show that for the 38,200 posters printed by the New York City project that year, supplies (including paint, linseed oil, varnish, silk organdy, petroleum jelly, turpentine, lacquer film, alcohol, and naptha) cost a scant $753. And there were additional reasons for their blossoming: the FAP had been in place for several years and most of the logistics of the program had been worked out; government agencies were learning about the availability of the posters; the art projects in general were proving themselves successful.

Thus, by 1938 WPA/FAP poster divisions existed in at least eighteen states, including California, Michigan, Minnesota, Ohio, Illinois, and Pennsylvania (whose division also produced lithograph and woodblock posters) [138-140, 303, 304]. FAP poster artists were being called upon to create posters for bulletin boards, school and community centers, buses, and subways. Some posters advertised civic activities, band concerts, lectures, and Federal Theatre Project productions; others informed citizens about health-care problems and treatment centers; poster divisions even produced some book jackets for Federal Writers Project publications and covers for FAP exhibition catalogs. In Los Angeles, the regional office of the Federal Theatre Project produced posters for productions in that city and in San Diego, Portland, and Seattle. Chicago had two poster units whose combined production capabilities enabled them to produce 1,500 posters a day at a production cost of 10 cents apiece, a bargain price even in the Depression. The Chicago units—second in productivity only to the one in New York—produced 600,000 posters from 1936 to 1940 for over 60 different city

■

and state agencies, including the Tennessee Valley Authority, the Federal Theatre Project, the Chicago Board of Education, and the U.S. departments of public health, conservation, agriculture, rural electrification, and employment.

A New Golden Age

Even more compelling than the volume was the extraordinary quality of the pieces being turned out by the WPA/FAP poster divisions. These artists and printers were truly creating a new golden age because they were bringing the high aesthetic standards of fine art to poster design—and getting noticed for it. "Sheer numerical production may sound impressive, as it surely does in this case, but if it were not for the amazing design quality invested in these posters, which has raised them to the status of a true art form, there would be no particular interest in them," noted Sidney Kellner, formerly with the Detroit Institute of Arts, in a 1938 issue of the trade journal **Signs of the Times**. "The professional scorn, which has been entertained generally by the 'fine' artist for the work of his brother, the 'commercial' artist, seems to have been swept away by the constant barrage of good posters turned out by the WPA Federal Art Project." A number of FAP galleries held exhibitions devoted to poster art [38–41], and the shows were taken seriously: **The New York Times** praised a 1938 show of posters from the New York City, Rochester, and New Jersey divisions [239], saying, "A high average is maintained, indicating distinct and most gratifying progress in the field."

Why a new golden age under the auspices of government sponsorship, which one might expect would restrict rather than free the artist's imagination? Interestingly, it was precisely because the poster division's clients were government agencies that the artists were able to approach their work in bold, experimental ways. Unlike designers working for advertising agencies, these poster artists were under no

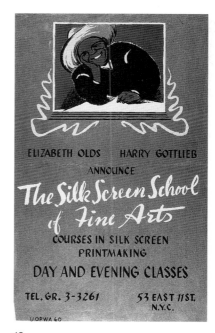

18
This poster by FAP participant Elizabeth Olds advertised the first school devoted to the art of silkscreening.

pressure to produce copy and imagery meant to hype some advertiser's product. The poster division's government clients had no anxiety about whether their message was producing profits; they were merely interested in providing basic information about public events and services. Extremely pleased with the high quality and low cost of the work produced on their behalf, they only rarely had complaints about execution or content.

Consequently, these artists experienced an unprecedented freedom to experiment with typography, colors, visual styles, and techniques. They took excellent advantage of this freedom. Keenly aware of developments in the fine arts, the poster division artists' work was often stylistically years ahead of that produced by commercial firms, freely applying concepts of design derived from abstract, Constructivist, and Bauhaus principles. Their knowledge of international developments in the art of poster design is also evident, as many of the WPA posters incorporate elements derived from the work of noted European and American poster artists, including Joseph Binder [153, 154], Otis Shepard [200], E. McKnight-Kauffer [71], and A.M. Cassandre [6]. The WPA/FAP printers, too, experimented and developed such skills that, for example, in 1940 the New York City poster division was chosen to produce a Binder-designed poster for the government-sponsored National Art Week [25].

Indeed, so far ahead of their commercial counterparts were the WPA poster artists that when they re-entered mainstream commercial art, their efforts to apply concepts they had used regularly in their WPA art were at first resisted. "When I tried to introduce some of the design concepts to the advertising world," remembers Jerry Roth [306], "I was hushed up, turned down, and turned off, because they felt it was too modern and avant-garde for the advertising profession." It was only "gradually, in time," he says, that "these ideas were absorbed."

19
Catalogue cover for the first group exhibition of silkscreen prints, sponsored by the Springfield Museum of Fine Arts in 1940.

One man responsible for bringing outstanding design sensibility to the FAP's posters was Richard Floethe [20, 281]. Floethe was already an internationally known industrial designer and book illustrator before he took over from John Weaver as administrator of the New York City poster division in 1936. As a student in Germany, he had trained at the Bauhaus, the progressive, influential design school founded by Walter Gropius; there he had studied design with Paul Klee and color theory and composition with Wassily Kandinsky. Floethe's background is reflected in the designs produced by the New York City division under his tutelage [132, 141].

As important as his Bauhaus training, however, was Floethe's rare and strikingly democratic organizational talent. Floethe felt that the government, by forming the poster divisions to provide employment for jobless commercial artists, had "unwittingly launched a movement to improve the commercial poster and raise it to a true art form," and he set out to exploit this situation to the fullest. Rather than simply assigning tasks to be executed, Floethe encouraged and stimulated the artists working under him, creating an atmosphere in which they felt free to experiment. When a new assignment arose, for example, Floethe would open it to competition. Specifications for topic, size, and content would be posted, and anyone in the division could submit preliminary sketches for consideration [12]. This healthy competition resulted in artists stretching their imaginations, generating a wide range of ideas, and taking pride in their work. Floethe also encouraged collaboration and interaction—a spirit that was common among most of the WPA art projects. The effectiveness of the posters produced during Floethe's tenure resulted in more orders than could be filled; consequently, his artists always had new projects on which to work.

20
Richard Floethe, Bauhaus graduate and administrator of the N.Y.C. poster division, is shown (circa 1938) working on a poster design from his sketches.

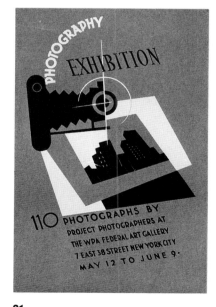

21
An exhibition catalogue cover based on a poster designed by Anthony Velonis [315].

The Decline of the Federal Art Project

Despite its numerous achievements, the FAP faced ongoing challenges to its existence. Opposition to work relief projects had existed in Congress from the earliest days of Roosevelt's New Deal Administration. Certainly to those congressional representatives who believed that WPA workers were engaged in nothing but "boondoggling" and "shovel leaning," providing salaries to artists seemed like "make work" in the extreme. Typical were such sentiments as those of Representative J. Parnell Thomas, who went on record calling the Federal Writers Project "a hot bed for Communists," and of Representative Dewey Short, who made his point on the floor of Congress that true art was the product of suffering artists while "subsidized art is no art at all."

In fact, by 1936 congressional opposition to WPA projects had become so strong that hundreds of New York City FAP artists staged demonstrations in response to widespread rumors that the art projects were being ended. The rumors proved untrue, but the signals pointing toward extinction increased: in 1937, for example, the regulations issued for the FAP required a 25 percent reduction in personnel, and artists again protested by staging sit-ins and work stoppages for several months, though they didn't succeed in having the policy rescinded. And in July 1937, Washington added a new regulation stating that noncitizens could not be employed by the WPA, which led to a significant drop in the number of artists that the programs employed.

Congressional opposition to the work relief concept was only one obstacle that the FAP artists faced. In Washington there were longheld beliefs that the WPA projects were riddled with "subversive"— that is, left-leaning—elements. In April 1939 the House Investigative Committee, headed by Representative Martin Dies, began questioning FAP workers regarding union and political activities. Citing political demonstrations by FAP workers [23, 24], organizing efforts by artists involved with the American Artists' Congress, and the employment of artists regarded as leftist, the Dies committee was determined to gather congressional and public support for complete elimination of the programs.

For months the Dies committee garnered headlines and notoriety with its activities. In its motives and tactics, it was a frightening precursor to the McCarthyism of the 1950s. The committee successfully persuaded Congress, for example, to kill the Federal Theatre Project, America's first and only national theater. Unlike, say, music or dance, whose content can be hard to pin down, the obvious social commentary being put forth in words and deeds in some (though by no means all) of the Federal Theatre Project plays was too much for the commitee to accept.

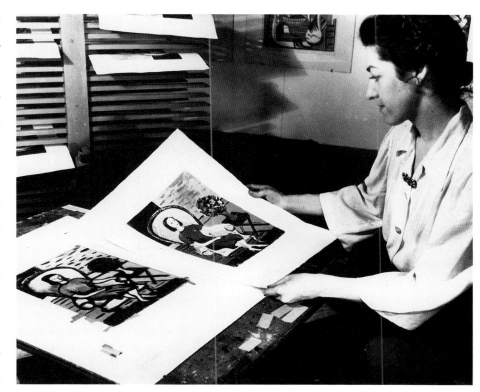

22
FAP Printmaker Ruth Chaney compares her original sketch (left) with finished serigraph, **Girl in Gray**, 1940.

The sad irony was that all the congressional hysteria was unfounded; the FAP was never rampant with reds, as the committee's actions suggest. Artists encompassed the wide spectrum of political thought typical of American society as a whole. While artists with Communist and other radical beliefs were certainly employed on the projects, neither by number nor by influence were they directing policy or programs. The 1930s, after all, was a time of social and political turmoil in America, and leftists politics were not outside the mainstream. These philosophies merely reflected a strong, native-grown, populist strain that, in the best tradition of American progressive thought, attempted

■

23
The scene at a rally called in January 1937 at Madison Square Garden to protest cutbacks of WPA programs. Placards carried by protesters were silkscreened by WPA printers in their off-project hours.

bold new solutions to pressing problems. The hopeful, liberal belief that citizens' lives could be made better by government action was its public manifestation.

The country was struggling with the dilemma of the Depression and its resultant social dislocations. Unemployment, public health, public housing, and job training were issues addressed not only by government policymakers but by artists both on and off the FAP. For instance, the Social Realist movement in art, which flourished during the WPA's time, was an attempt by artists to direct public awareness to such issues. And, like the Social Realists, the WPA/FAP poster artists were making valuable contributions to public awareness. Many of the strongest and most effective poster designs dealt with public health and education; venereal disease, for example, was a prime concern of public health agencies, but at the time simply mentioning the subject in a public forum was a bold step. The title of one poster, **Shame May Be Fatal** [8], effectively underscores a prevalent New Deal philosophy: Problems will not be solved by inattention; they must be confronted in order to be overcome.

To conservative and reactionary forces in and out of Congress, however, artists' work was suspect precisely because it dealt with social issues. That the government would involve itself with the arts seemed not only financially wasteful but politically extreme. Murals were searched for Communist iconography, and Federal Theatre Project plays (before their demise) were attacked for their alleged political content. O'Connor and Brown's history of the FTP, **Free, Adult, Uncensored**, relates the story of one attack, a children's play—**Revolt of the Beavers**, in which a group of beavers acts together to resolve problems stemming from a mean boss beaver—was viewed by critics as Marxism veiled in Mother Goose and as a result of the controversy was closed down by FTP administrators. These much-publicized red hunts, though unsuccessful in actually turning up Communist influence, have tainted the work of the FAP to this day, obscuring the vital contributions the projects made both to the arts and to the public.

24
3,000 WPA workers representing twenty-four states marched on the Capitol and the White House in 1936 seeking expansion of government work-relief programs.

The head of the New York City WPA projects, Colonel Brehon Somervell, was a classic example of the conservative attitude of the time. An imperious, impeccably groomed career military man who was described by **Time** as "dynamite in a Tiffany box," Somervell seemed in all ways an inappropriate choice to administer art projects. "As a painter, I'm a good bricklayer," he once responded to a reporter who questioned him regarding the merits of a painting. Somervell's appointment was based on his reputed performance as a no-nonsense administrator of funds, not on his love of the arts. He felt it was his professional and personal duty to "clean [the art projects] up," as he told his director of the NYC / FAP, Audrey McMahon.

Artist Anthony Velonis remembers being appointed by Somervell to a committee to, as Velonis recalls the colonel's words, "separate the good artists from the bad artists." Many who were asked to serve on this committee were former FAP artists who were initially unaware of the colonel's private "clean up" agenda. But at the very first meeting, as it became clear that arbitrary standards were being set up in order to find reasons to fire people, a group of artists left the meeting en masse. They later issued a signed statement resigning from the committee and protesting the removal of artists from FAP work; among the artists who resigned were Velonis, Stuart Davis, Raphael Soyer, Hyman Warsager, and Will Barnet. "We simply didn't want to be used as a firing squad," commented Harry Sternberg. But the resignations backfired: those who resigned were replaced by people who shared Somervell's views, and the colonel wound up with a free hand to impose his standards.

By 1938, when a proposal limiting the FAP artists' annual salaries to $1,000 was advanced, it became apparent that the Federal Art Projects were headed toward extinction. In order to retain government funding, the arts projects had to be supported with at least 25 percent of their total operating budget from local sources. This led to drastic reductions in the number of functioning arts centers as economic conditions made it difficult for municipalities to provide financing. Another major blow was passage in 1939 of the "18-month

25

Printers at work producing a Joseph Binder design for National Art Week, a 1940 government-sponsored program that encouraged the public to purchase low-cost, original American art.

rule," which limited artists to 18 months of employment. In New York City, passage of this rule, immediately removed 70 percent of the artists from WPA programs.

By late 1939, some projects had closed down altogether; those that remained had been forced to curtail their activities severely. The once-vital New York City FAP remained alive only because Mayor La Guardia placed it under city sponsorship. The city's poster division continued to produce, although with continually dwindling staff numbers.

In 1942, after the United States entered World War II and the nation's energies turned in a new direction, the Federal Art Projects was transferred to Defense Department sponsorship and renamed the Graphics Section of the War Service Division. Under this new sponsorship, the government-employed poster artists produced training aids, airport plans, rifle sight charts, silhouettes of German and Japanese aircraft, "Buy Bonds" booths [260], and patriotic posters such as one designed to encourage homefront knitting: "Remember Pearl Harbor—Purl Harder." Artists who had been using silkscreen to create prints and posters now worked on menus for officers' mess halls, camp insignias, and window displays. These works were rougher, less well designed, than the prewar pieces, but at least they did maintain the FAP tradition of creating art in service to the public. (One addition to the staff—after being dropped from the FAP easel painting division—was Jackson Pollock. He and fellow abstract artists Lee Krasner and Ben Benn worked for the window display project, a division that created informational displays about war-related educational activities that were being offered to civilians in New York City colleges.)

But by this time the WPA art projects were clearly diminished. More and more, the nation's resources were being directed to the war effort; in addition, unemployment—which the WPA programs had originally been created to ease—virtually disappeared in the

26
As need increased for civilian workers during World War II, poster artists devoted more time to producing military signage, training aids, and other homefront-related items.

■

booming wartime economy. All projects were phased out in mid 1943 and, in keeping with the tenor of the times, Roosevelt declared that the WPA had served with distinction and "earned its honorable discharge."

The Fate of the WPA Posters

No central federal repository had been established for storing the WPA's records, so as they closed, many WPA agencies trashed any paperwork and materials on hand. By regulation, works created by WPA artists could not be sold, so those pieces that were not allocated to educational institutions or museums were frequently tossed out. Often artworks and records survived only because project workers with a personal interest in them saved them from an inglorious end in the dump. The fate met by the paintings of the New York City FAP easel section in 1944 was typical: nine years' worth of fine artwork was sold as scrap-by-the-pound to a Long Island salvage dealer. Luckily—and this was not typical—a Lower West Side curio shop owner discovered the sale, bought the canvases [29], and informed his artist friends. They were able to buy back many of their works at prices averaging $3 to $5 per painting and $25 apiece for the larger mural studies. The shop owner also based his prices on size, not aesthetic quality or artistic importance.

Posters, being by nature ephemera intended for short-term use, were even less likely than paintings to be salvaged. Indeed, the fate of the poster divisions' output is largely unknown. Some 500 posters for the Federal Theatre Project were located in 1973 among the FTP's records stored in a Baltimore airplane hangar, where they had been unexamined for 30 years; they now form part of the FTP collection of George Mason University. Approximately 900 posters were allocated to the Library of Congress between 1938 and 1941, but none have entered since, and the collection was only rediscovered and acces-sioned in 1966. The Chicago Historical Society holds 40 posters in its

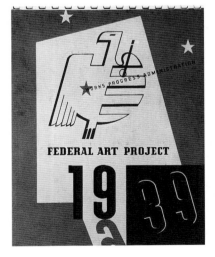

27
This calendar was produced by eight artists of the N.Y.C. poster division [316]. Cover design by Jerome Roth.

print collection; the Cleveland Public Library collection contains 20 posters; and the New York Historical Society has only five posters in its Graphics Division. By best estimates, slightly over 2,000 posters remain in known collections. This represents a mere one-tenth of one percent of the total number produced.

Despite the fact that they were ephemera, the extent of the posters' anonymity is surprising, particularly given the vast numbers in which they were produced during the WPA period. Today, at a time of continually increasing interest in the art of the poster, many poster dealers and collectors throughout the nation have never seen any of the poster divisions' works, nor have they any knowledge of the posters' existence.

The works remain largely undocumented in any written history of poster art, and with the exception of an article published in **Print** in 1978, virtually no periodical since the FAP's demise has published them.* Even the collection's guardian, the Library of Congress, seemed unaware of its holding for many years. In an introduction to a catalog for a 1967 Smithsonian Institution-circulated exhibition of American posters, exhibition curator Edgar Breitenbach, chief of the Library of Congress Prints and Photographs division, wrote that the half-century between 1917 and 1967 "has been shrouded in silence. It is my purpose here to attempt to rescue this chapter of American art from oblivion, and to pay [American] poster artists a tribute which is long

28
The Strike is Won, a 1938 serigraph, celebrates the successful conclusion to a Pennsylvania miners' strike. It was created by Harry Gottlieb, an original member of the silkscreen group established in the graphic art division of the FAP.

*In 1986 articles were written by the author about these posters and they appeared in **Communication Arts** and **I.D.** magazines.

29
New York curio shop owner Henry Roberts exhibits one of hundreds of FAP easel paintings he offered for sale at prices from $3.00 to $25.00 in 1944. He obtained the pictures from a Long Island scrap dealer who had purchased a job lot of "junk canvas" at a government surplus sale.

overdue." But this "tribute" makes no mention of the posters of the WPA. Either Breitenbach felt the WPA posters were of little aesthetic value, or —what's more likely—he was simply unaware of their existence.

It is perhaps because of the lowly status unfairly accorded WPA art in general that these poster works have been undervalued for so long. Tainted during the WPA's life as "boondoggle art," quickly filed away and forgotten as America entered World War II, and almost completely buried during the anti-Communist hysteria of the 1950s, the work of the WPA artists has only recently begun to be rediscovered. Its long-overdue reevaluation is finally being undertaken. Exhibitions of WPA art (though none devoted solely to the art of the poster) have been mounted in recent years by the National Gallery of Art, numerous universities, and private galleries across the country. Efforts such as these will prove important in changing the perception of WPA artworks by critics, collectors, and the public, whose familiarity with the works—if any—is filtered through nearly 50 years of neglect and misrepresentation.

Whatever the factor that have kept these works hidden, one fact is clear: The posters represent the work of talented and skilled artists producing in a collaborative, stimulating environment, fueled by a system formed specifically to allow artists the freedom to create during the depths of the Great Depression. These posters show consistently excellent design and workmanship. The WPA posters are a significant part of our national art heritage, and although they have slipped into obscurity, they deserve to be seen again.

30
Artist unknown
Boston, MA
56 x 36 cm.
22 x 14 in.

31
Katherine Milhous
Philadelphia, PA
61 x 47 cm.
24 x 18½ in.
Woodblock

Federal Art Project Posters

The posters that the WPA/FAP artists created to promote FAP activities represent
some of their most accomplished work. These
posters, after all, reflect the pride that the
artists felt in their special field of endeavor.

The FAP's activities were designed not merely to employ
artists but to expand the audience for art. Thus, for example, at a time
when the majority of Americans had never seen an oil painting or visited
a museum, WPA/FAP Community Art Centers in 103 cities allowed eight
million people to view works of art and attend studio classes. The WPA/
FAP artists created posters to inform the public of these opportunities.

Other art-related activities sponsored by the FAP included the Design Laboratory, which was based on Bauhaus philosophy
and created to teach how fine arts principles could be applied to
industrial design, and the Paint Testing and Research Laboratory operated by the Massachusetts FAP, from which emerged a Bureau of Standards code for specifications of artists' materials.

The art of printmaking enjoyed a renaissance as FAP artists
produced woodblock prints, etchings, monotypes, and linoleum block
prints. Several new printmaking processes were developed in FAP
graphic arts workshops, including experimental techniques in stone
lithography, the medium of the serigraph (based on techniques evolved
in making silkscreened posters), and the carborundum print (a process
in which an abrasive powder is used to add texture to a lithographic
stone). Art activities such as these were brought to the attention of the
public through FAP-sponsored exhibitions and through posters created
by the WPA / FAP artists.

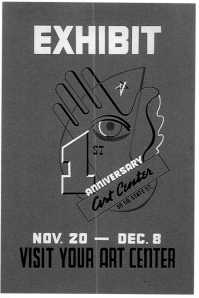

32
Artist unknown
Salt Lake City, UT
56 x 36 cm.
22 x 14 in.

33
These posters on display at the 1939
exhibition "New Horizons in American
Art" at the M.H. DeYoung Museum, San
Francisco, showcase the works of poster
artists from Pennsylvania and New York
[116, 132, 138, 228, 304].

■

34
Ben Nason
(attributed)
Boston, MA
63 x 46 cm.
24¾ x 18 in.

35
Ben Nason
(attributed)
Boston, MA
63 x 46 cm.
24¾ x 18 in.

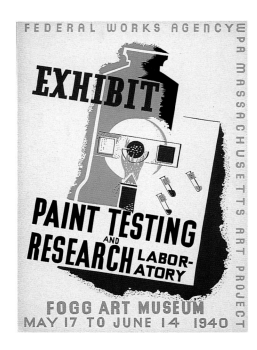

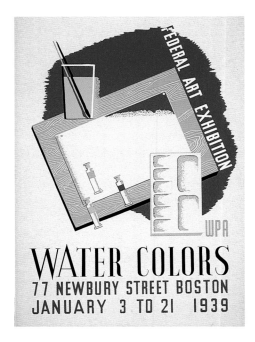

36
H.G. (signed)
Boston, MA
56 x 36 cm.
22 x 14 in.

37
Artist unknown
Boston, MA
56 x 36 cm.
22 x 14 in.

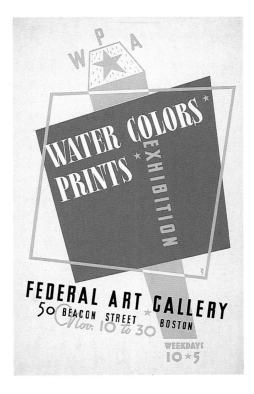

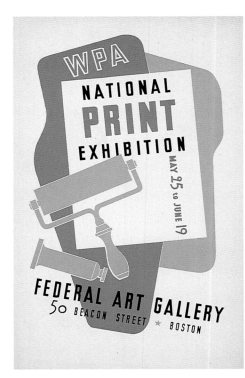

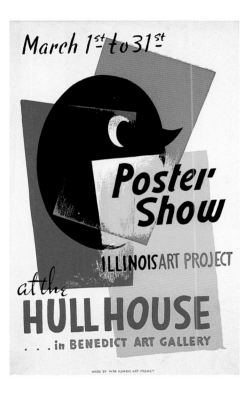

38
Stanley T. Clough
Cleveland, OH
56 x 36 cm.
22 x 14 in.

39
Artist unknown
Chicago, IL
56 x 36 cm.
22 x 14 in.

Although the New York City Federal Art Project employed the largest number of artists, most major urban centers had active WPA art units. At the zenith of their activities in 1938, poster design units operated in eighteen states. These "posters about posters" attest to the skills of designers nationally.

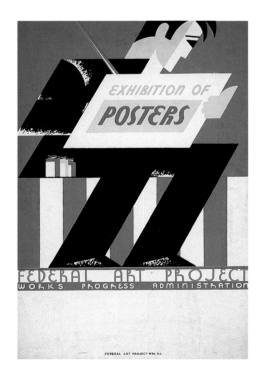

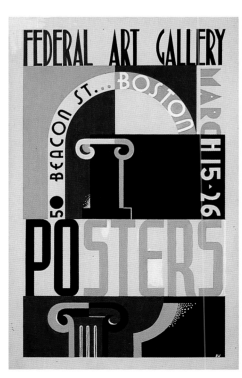

40
Artist unknown
Chicago, IL
76 x 51 cm.
30 x 20 in.

41
Russell W. West
Boston, MA
56 x 36 cm.
22 x 14 in.

42
Artist unknown
New York, NY
56 x 36 cm.
22 x 14 in.

43
Artist unknown
New York, NY
56 x 36 cm.
22 x 14 in.

44
Jerome Roth
(Rothstein)
New York, NY
56 x 36 cm.
22 x 14 in.

45
Artist unknown
Pittsburgh, PA
48 x 35 cm.
19 x 13¾ in.
Lithograph

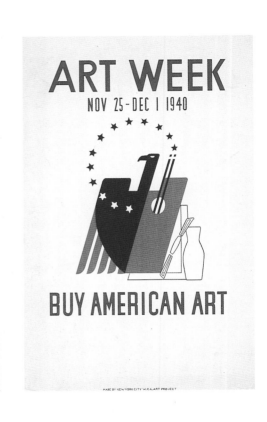

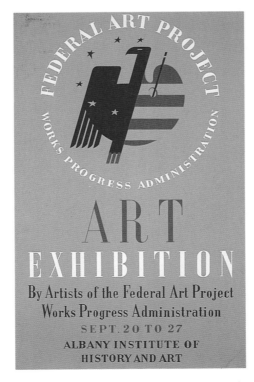

46
Artist unknown
Location unknown
91.5 x 63.5 cm.
36 x 25 in.

The eagle and palette logo of the Federal Art Project was never standardized. These five posters illustrate some of the many variations created.

47
Richard Floethe
New York, NY
36 x 56 cm.
14 x 22 in.

■

48
Artist unknown
Chicago, IL
76 x 51 cm.
30 x 20 in.

49
Artist unknown
New York, NY
56 x 36 cm.
22 x 14 in.

Government-sponsored easel painters produced over 100,000 paintings between 1935 and 1943. Among the artists employed were Jackson Pollock, Alice Neel, Lee Krasner, Jacob Lawrence, Ad Reinhardt, and Willem de Kooning. Many of the works were lost or destroyed when the WPA ended.

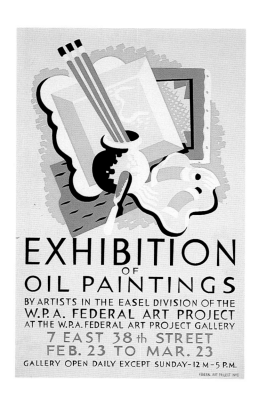

50
Richard Floethe
New York, NY
56 x 36 cm.
22 x 14 in.

51
Stanley T. Clough
Cleveland, OH
56 x 36 cm.
22 x 14 in.

52
Erel Osborn
Chicago, IL
56 x 36 cm.
22 x 14 in.

53
Artist unknown
Chicago, IL
56 x 36 cm.
22 x 14 in.

Children's art education was a major
emphasis of the Community Art Centers
operated by the WPA in over 100 cities. In
addition to taking classes, children were
given the opportunity to exhibit their work.
Figures 54 and 56 are adaptations of young
people's art by poster artists.

54
George Vander Sluis
(Child's drawing
by Jack Wittrock
age 12)
Cleveland, OH
58 x 36 cm.
23 x 14 in.

55
E.T. (signed)
Chicago, IL
56 x 36 cm.
22 x 14 in.

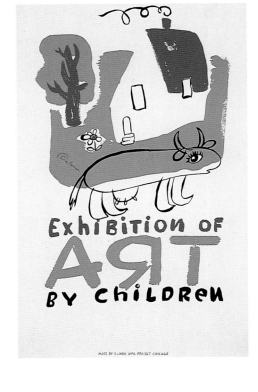

56
Artist unknown
Sioux City, IA
36 x 56 cm.
14 x 22 in.

57
Artist unknown
Boston, MA
56 x 36 cm.
22 x 14 in.

58
Ben Nason
Boston, MA
63 x 46 cm.
24¾ x 18 in.

As these posters show, many mediums
of artistic expression were encouraged
through WPA sponsorship. Printmakers
employed included Mabel Dwight, Will
Barnet, Harry Gottleib, Louis Lozowick, Fritz
Eichenberg, and Elizabeth Olds.

59
Arlington Gregg
Chicago, IL
56 x 36 cm.
22 x 14 in.

60
Stanley T. Clough
Cleveland, OH
56 x 36 cm.
22 x 14 in.

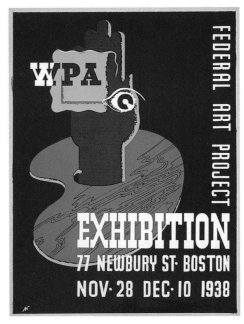

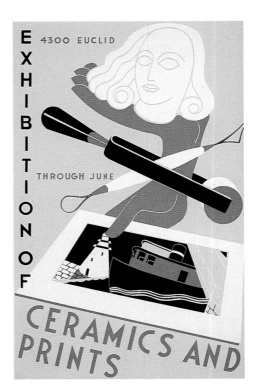

61
Erel Osborn
Chicago, IL
56 x 36 cm.
22 x 14 in.

62
Artist unknown
Boston, MA
66 x 43 cm.
26 x 17 in.

One of the most important and productive divisions of the FAP was the Index of American Design. It documented American craft and folk arts created from the Colonial period to the end of the nineteenth century. Artists using watercolors rendered 22,000 plates that recorded textiles, costumes, objects, and furniture. These plates now reside in the National Gallery of Art.

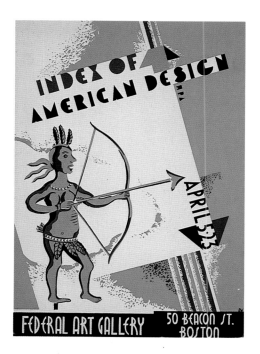

63
Artist unknown
Chicago, IL
76 x 51 cm.
30 x 20 in.

64
Russell W. West
Boston, MA
63 x 45 cm.
24¾ x 17¾ in.

65
Vera Bock
(attributed)
New York, NY
56 x 36 cm.
22 x 14 in.

This poster illustrates Maurice Glickman's sculpture **Destitute (Mother and Child)**.

■

66
Artist unknown
Chicago, IL
56 x 36 cm.
22 x 14 in.

67
Erel Osborn
Chicago, IL
56 x 36 cm.
22 x 14 in.

An interesting array of textural effects is obtained in these posters: sponged [67] and spatter [69]. A rare photo silkscreen [68] incorporates a work by Picasso printed by means of a photosensitive emulsion.

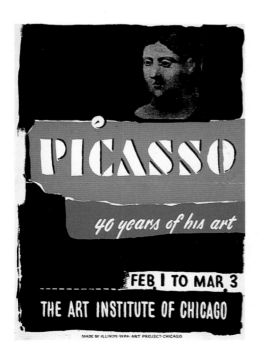

68
Artist unknown
Chicago, IL
36 x 25 cm.
14¼ x 9¾ in.

69
Angelo Tartaglia
Essex County, NJ
56 x 36 cm.
22 x 14 in.

70
B.F. (signed)
Sioux City, IA
36 x 56 cm.
4 x 22 in.

71
Artist unknown
Iowa
56 x 36 cm.
22 x 14 in.

72
B.F. (signed)
Sioux City, IA
71 x 56 cm.
28 x 22 in.

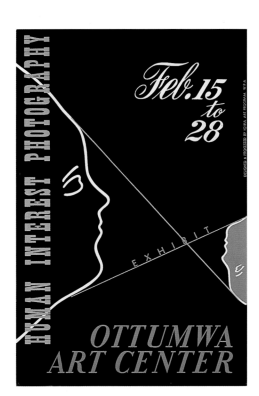

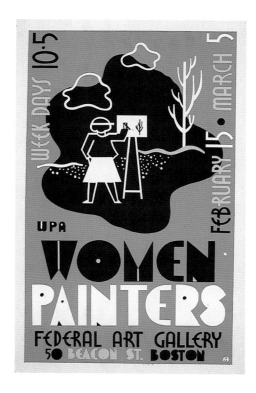

73
Russell W. West
Boston, MA
56 x 36 cm.
22 x 14 in.

74
Erel Osborn
Chicago, IL
56 x 36 cm.
22 x 14 in.

The WPA provided opportunities for many artists to exhibit their work. Women comprised forty-one percent of the artists employed by the Federal Art Project nationally. This surprisingly large number speaks encouragingly of the FAP's democratic vision [73].

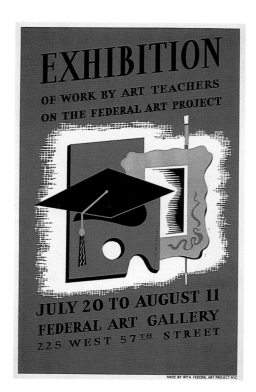

75
Anthony Velonis
New York, NY
56 x 36 cm.
22 x 14 in.

76
John Buczak
Chicago, IL
56 x 36 cm.
22 x 14 in.

77
Pistchal
(attributed)
New York, NY
56 x 36 cm.
22 x 14 in.

The central image on this poster is taken
from a Kiowa painted shield cover. The
original design was received in a vision
and shows a bear running out of clouds
into rows of flying bullets.

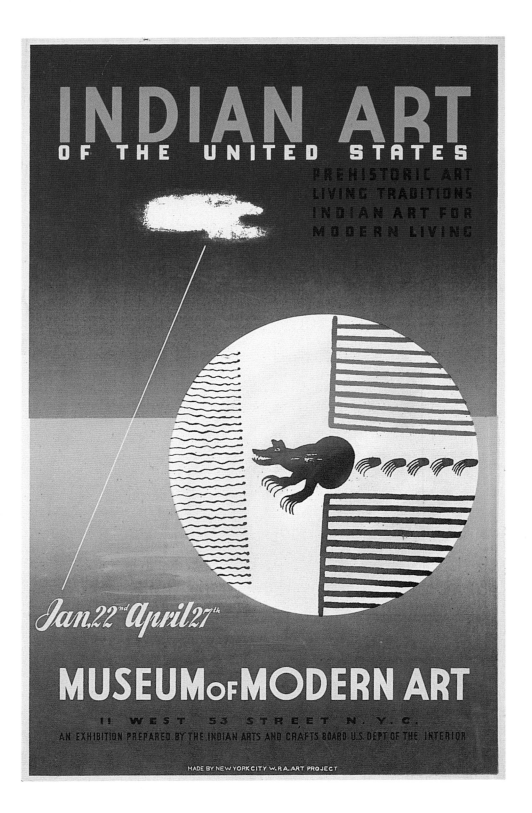

78
Pistchal
New York, NY
56 x 36 cm.
22 x 14 in.

The source for this poster design is a mica ornament from the Hopewell people of present-day Ohio.

79
Louis B. Siegriest
(Native American
art by Ha-So-Deh)
San Francisco, CA
86 x 57 cm.
34 x 23 in.

80
Louis B. Siegriest
(Native American
art by Chiuh Tah)
San Francisco, CA
86 x 57 cm.
34 x 23 in.

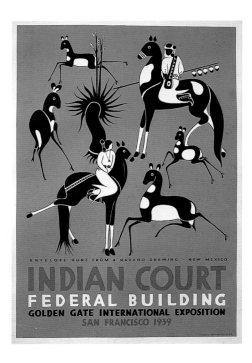

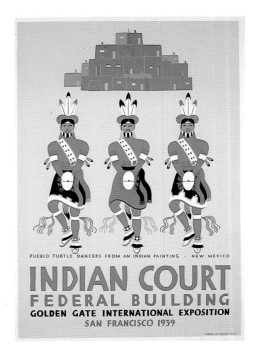

81–86
Louis B. Siegriest
(Native American
artists unknown)
San Francisco, CA
86 x 57 cm.
34 x 23 in.

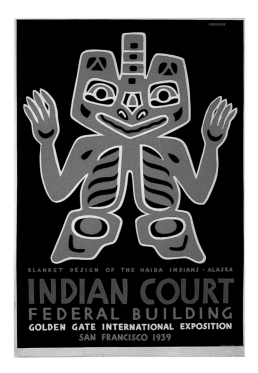

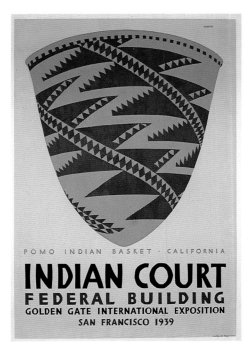

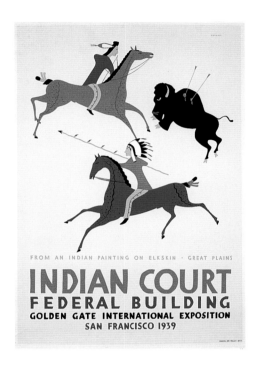

FROM AN INDIAN PAINTING ON ELKSKIN · GREAT PLAINS

INDIAN COURT
FEDERAL BUILDING
GOLDEN GATE INTERNATIONAL EXPOSITION
SAN FRANCISCO 1939

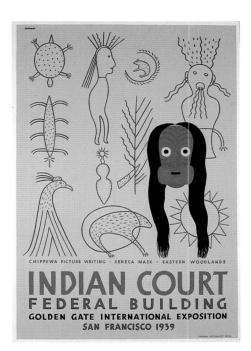

CHIPPEWA PICTURE WRITING · SENECA MASK · EASTERN WOODLANDS

INDIAN COURT
FEDERAL BUILDING
GOLDEN GATE INTERNATIONAL EXPOSITION
SAN FRANCISCO 1939

These eight **Indian Court** posters were designed for the 1939 Golden Gate International Exposition in San Francisco by Louis B. Siegriest. He had already made a major contribution to California painting as a member of the "Society of Six," the Oakland based group of plein air or outdoor artists of the 1920's, prior to his working for the WPA / FAP. For the year and a half of this employment, he was the sole artist on the Federal Art Project in San Francisco and during that time he designed the first **Indian Court** poster of a Pomo Indian basket. After Siegriest left the WPA, René Harnoncourt, then director of the Indian Arts and Crafts Boards of the U.S. Department of the Interior, and later director of the Museum of Modern Art, commissioned him to design the remaining seven posters. Siegriest selected images representing the Navaho, Pueblo, Haida, Plains, Chippewa, Seneca, Eskimo, and Apache tribal nations from reference materials supplied by Harnoncourt. The production of the posters was done by the WPA / FAP poster unit, housed in the lower level of a boat anchored off Treasure Island (site of the exposition), where Siegriest supervised the stencil cutting and silkscreening of his designs for worldwide distribution.

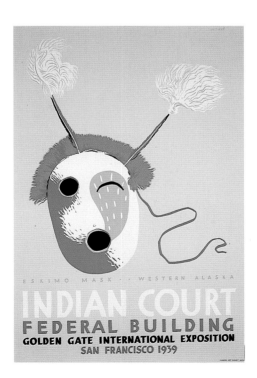

ESKIMO MASK · WESTERN ALASKA

INDIAN COURT
FEDERAL BUILDING
GOLDEN GATE INTERNATIONAL EXPOSITION
SAN FRANCISCO 1939

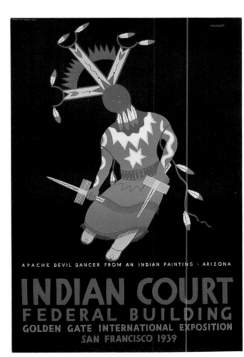

APACHE DEVIL DANCER FROM AN INDIAN PAINTING · ARIZONA

INDIAN COURT
FEDERAL BUILDING
GOLDEN GATE INTERNATIONAL EXPOSITION
SAN FRANCISCO 1939

■

87
Artist unknown
New York, NY
56 x 36 cm.
22 x 14 in.

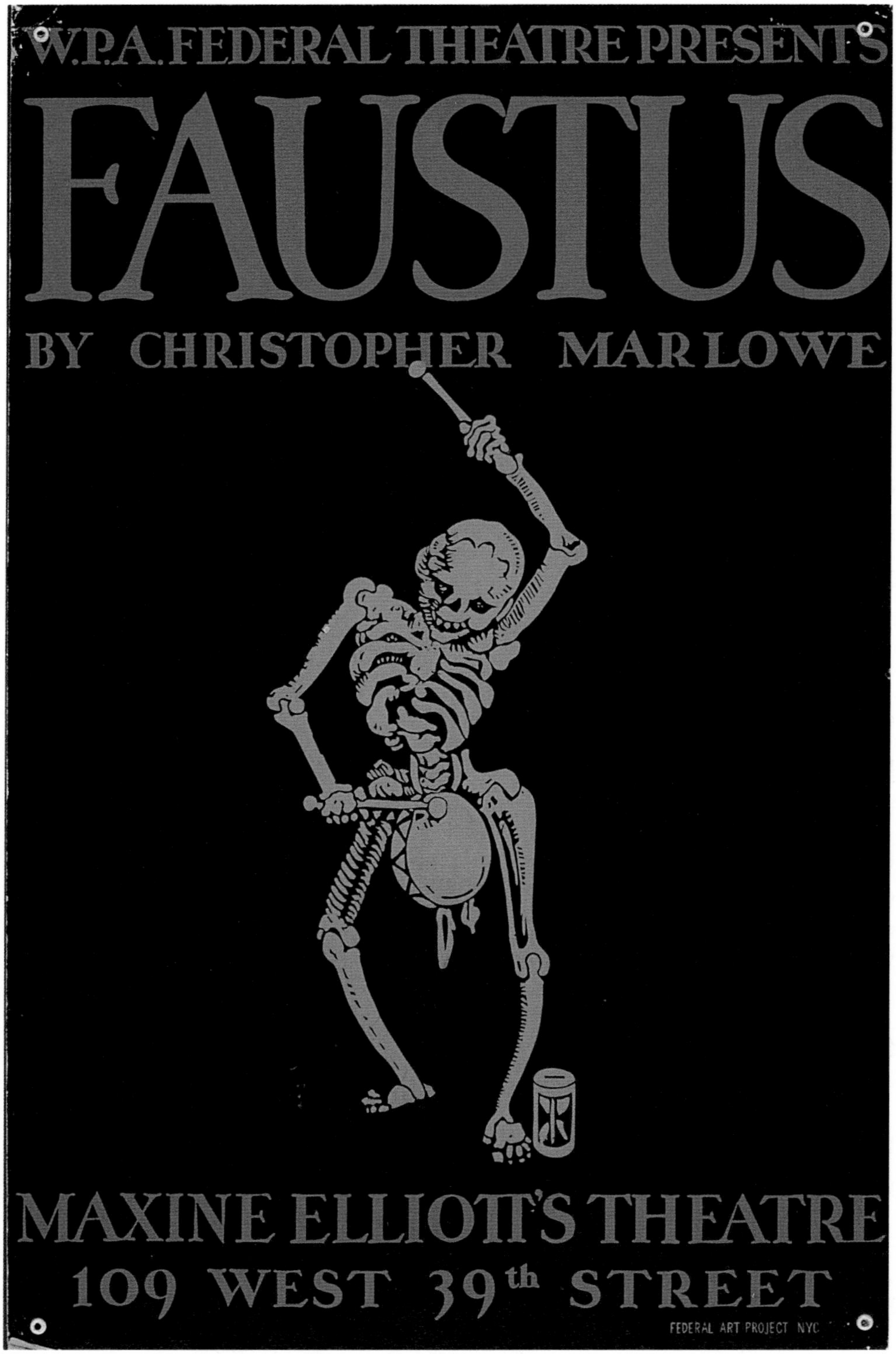

Faustus and **Macbeth**, two of the most successful FTP productions, were produced by John Houseman and directed by Orson Welles. **Macbeth** featured an all black cast, a score by Virgil Thomson, and its setting was changed to Haiti. This "Voodoo Shakespeare" ran seven months in New York and toured nationwide.

W.P.A. FEDERAL THEATRE PRESENTS

FAUSTUS

BY CHRISTOPHER MARLOWE

MAXINE ELLIOTT'S THEATRE
109 WEST 39th STREET

FEDERAL ART PROJECT NYC

Between 1935 and 1939, the Federal Theatre Project (FTP) flourished as the first and only government-sponsored and -subsidized theater program in our nation's history. Headed by Hallie Flanagan, the FTP was created to provide meaningful employment for theatrical professionals who, as Flanagan wrote, "could no longer live in America except on charity." In a mere four years, 150 FTP groups in 22 states employed 1,200 people and staged more than 2,700 productions viewed by audiences totaling over 25 million. Even a partial roll call of the talents nurtured by the FTP—Joseph Cotten, Jules Dassin, John Huston, Burt Lancaster, Joseph Losey, Sidney Lumet, Arthur Miller, Nicholas Ray, Virgil Thomson—speaks eloquently of its lasting contribution.

Beyond its successful ventures in such urban theatrical centers as New York, Chicago, Los Angeles, and Boston, the FTP brought performances to communities throughout the country that had never witnessed live theatrical presentations. Its repertoire was as varied as its audience—from revivals of dramatic classics (Shakespeare's **The Merry Wives of Windsor**, Marlowe's **Doctor Faustus**, and Shaw's **Androcles and the Lion**), to experimental new works such as the Living Newspaper.

Blacks, traditionally excluded from backstage craft unions, found employment and a creative outlet in the FTP's sixteen Negro Theatre Units. These productions included original works by black playwrights dealing with the first black republic, **Haiti**; folk history, **Run Little Chillun**; and racism in America, **Liberty Deferred**; as well as an adaptation of **Macbeth**, and the innovative **Swing Mikado**. The FTP also sponsored plays by Children's Theatre Units, the Federal Theatre Circus, and marionette units.

88
When this photo was taken in 1938, Orson Welles had already achieved success on the commercial Broadway stage. This poster for **Faustus**, Welles' first starring role, was hung in his office as a reminder of his earlier work with the Federal Theatre Project.

■

89
Emanuel DeColas
New York, NY
56 x 36 cm.
22 x 14 in.

90
Harry Herzog
New York, NY
56 x 36 cm.
22 x 14 in.

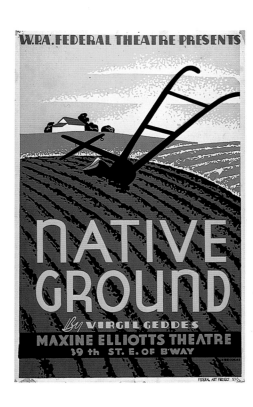

91
Artist unknown
New York, NY
56 x 36 cm.
22 x 14 in.

92
Irving Spellens
New York, NY
56 x 36 cm.
22 x 14 in.

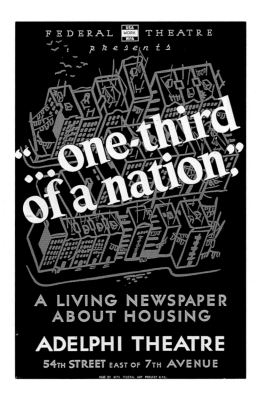

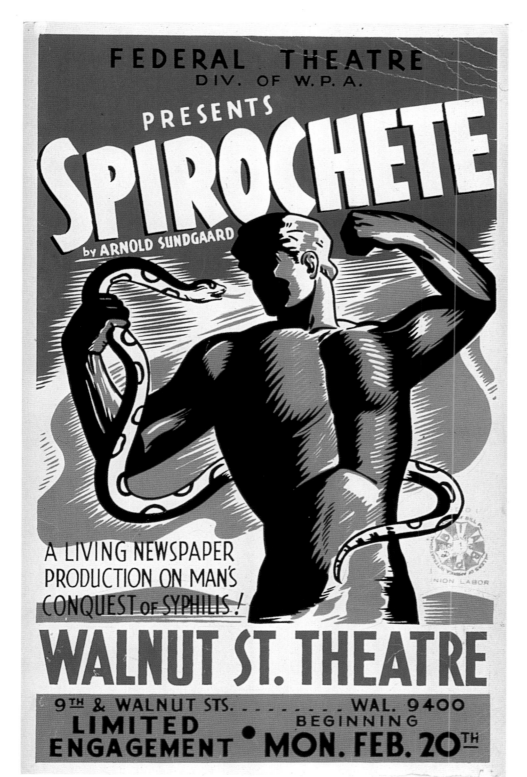

93
Artist unknown
Philadelphia, PA
56 x 36 cm.
22 x 14 in.

One division of the Federal Theater was the Living Newspaper which produced original dramas dealing with social issues of the day. The topics included here are slum housing [92], the plight of the small farmer [89], the need for rural electrification [91], and the history of American labor [90].

94
Charles Verschuuren
New York, NY
56 x 36 cm.
22 x 14 in.

95
Martin Weitzman
(attributed)
New York, NY
56 x 36 cm.
22 x 14 in.

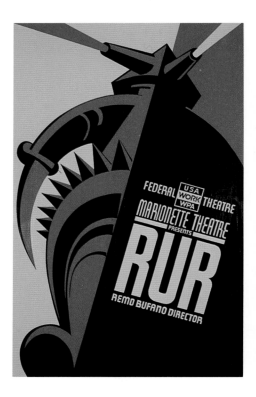

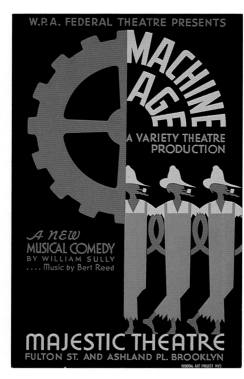

96
Herbert Pratt
New York, NY
56 x 36 cm.
22 x 14 in.

97
Artist unknown
New York, NY
56 x 36 cm.
22 x 14 in.

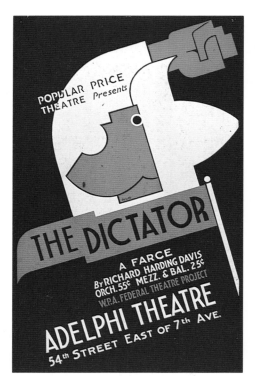

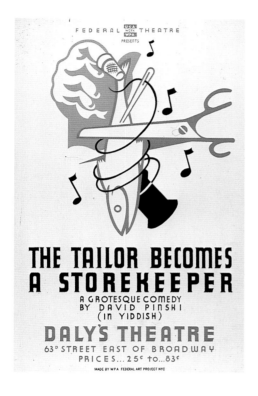

98
Artist unknown
New York, NY
56 x 36 cm.
22 x 14 in.

99
Artist unknown
San Francisco, CA
56 x 36 cm.
22 x 14 in.

The Federal Theatre produced many musicals and comedies. **Sing for Your Supper** introduced the John LaTouche / Earl Robinson song, "Ballad for Americans," made famous later by Paul Robeson.

100
Artist unknown
San Francisco, CA
56 x 36 cm.
22 x 14 in.

101
Aida McKenzie
New York, NY
56 x 36 cm.
22 x 14 in.

■

102
Harry Reminick
Columbus, OH
56 x 36 cm.
22 x 14 in.

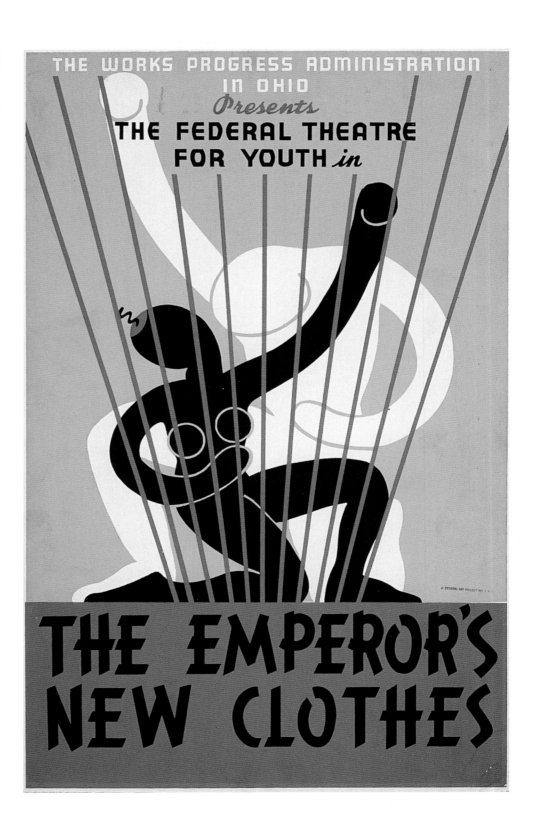

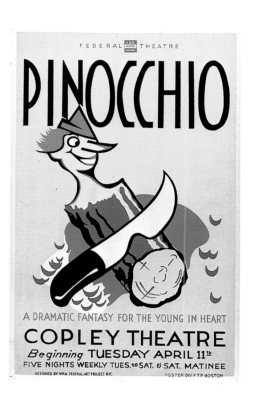

103
Richard Halls
(attributed)
New York, NY
56 x 36 cm.
22 x 14 in.

104
Artist unknown
New York, NY &
Boston, MA
56 x 36 cm.
22 x 14 in.

Across the country the Federal Theatre Project produced works for children. When Congress cut off all funds for the FTP in 1939, the New York troupe added a sad and bitter comment in their last performance of **Pinocchio**: As the play ended, the puppet hero was not allowed to come to life and stage hands demolished the set in view of the audience.

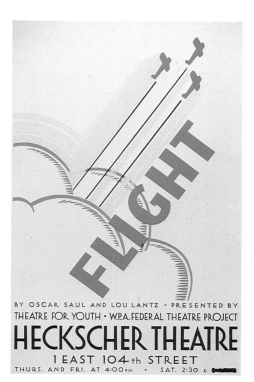

105
Artist unknown
New York, NY
56 x 36 cm.
22 x 14 in.

106
Artist unknown
Seattle, WA
56 x 36 cm.
22 x 14 in.

107
Anthony Velonis
New York, NY
56 x 36 cm.
22 x 14 in.

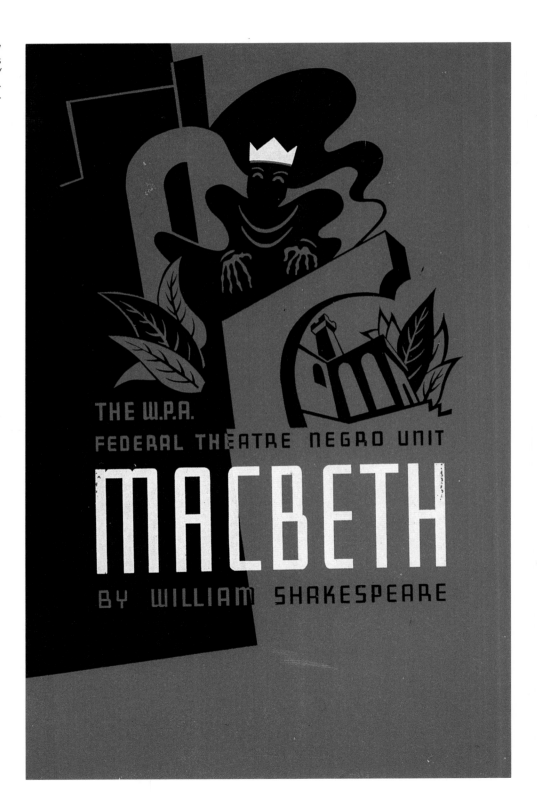

108
Artist unknown
New York, NY
56 x 36 cm.
22 x 14 in.

The marionette production **RUR** [94, 108] was based on a work by Karel Čapek of the same name, which introduced the word robot to the English language.

109
Artist unknown
Los Angeles, CA
107 x 71 cm.
42 x 28 in.

110
Harry Herzog
New York, NY
56 x 36 cm.
22 x 14 in.

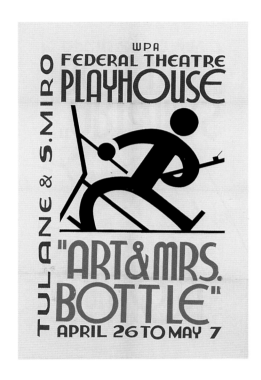

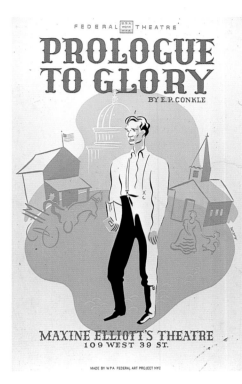

111
Artist unknown
St. Louis, MO
56 x 36 cm.
22 x 14 in.

112
Artist unknown
Boston, MA
56 x 36 cm.
22 x 14 in.

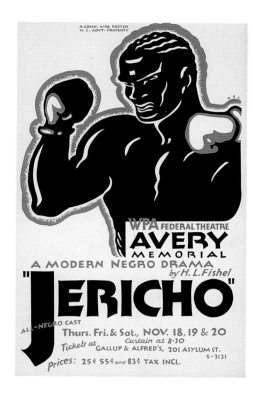

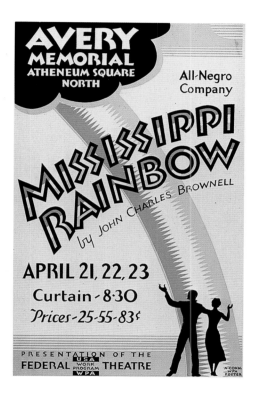

113
A.E.L. (signed)
Connecticut
56 x 36 cm.
22 x 14 in.

114
A.E.L. (attributed)
Connecticut
56 x 36 cm.
22 x 14 in.

The Negro Theatre Unit of the Federal
Theatre Project provided training for black
theatrical professionals as both performers
and technicians. After the demise of the
FTP, there was no widespread resurgence
of black theater troupes until the 1960s.

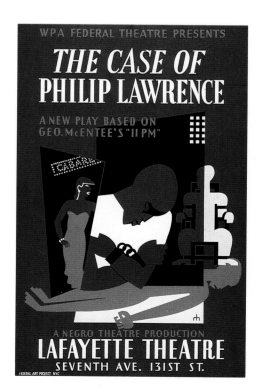

115
Richard Halls
New York, NY
56 x 36 cm.
22 x 14 in.

116
Vera Bock
New York, NY
56 x 36 cm.
22 x 14 in.

117
Ben Lassen
New York, NY
56 x 36 cm.
22 x 14 in.

FTP units presented many classic dramas.
George Bernard Shaw personally approved
discounted royalty payments so the FTP
could stage his works.

118
Artist unknown
Location unknown
28 x 53 cm.
11 x 21 in.

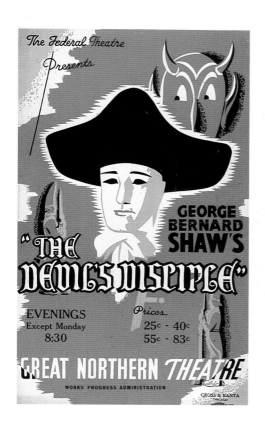

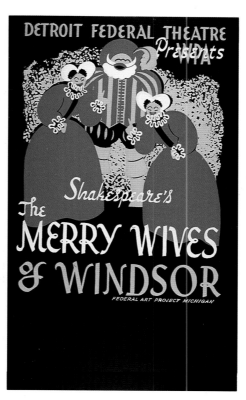

119
Artist unknown
Chicago, IL
56 x 36 cm.
22 x 14 in.

120
Artist unknown
Detroit, MI
56 x 36 cm.
22 x 14 in.

121
Artist unknown
Boston, MA
Preliminary design
mixed medium

122
Artist unknown
Boston, MA
Preliminary design
mixed medium

These preliminary sketches show four different approaches to the design of a poster. The final printed design [125] incorporates a bolder type plan, suitable for its advertising function, and a more stylized linear illustration.

123
Artist unknown
Boston, MA
Preliminary design
mixed medium

124
Artist unknown
Boston, MA
Preliminary design
mixed medium

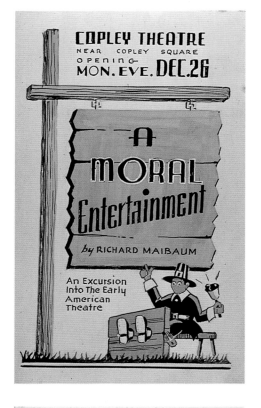

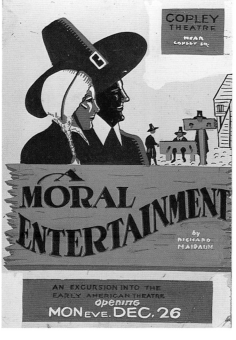

125
Artist unknown
Boston, MA
56 x 36 cm.
22 x 14 in.

■

A Remembrance of the WPA
by Anthony Velonis

The golden years of the WPA New York Federal Art Project were about four— from 1935 to 1939—the years, naturally, when I was employed by the "Project."

They seem golden to me now, loaded with nostalgia. That was another life and I am now another person, living a different life. Some of us remember our grandparents or even a great-grandmother. It is with that kind of distance in time that I now remember the project. Recently I unearthed some of the sketches of that period and remarked to myself, somewhat surprised by the young man's ability, as though it were someone else's work, "Not bad, not bad at all!" A little choke of wistfulness comes over me at what might have been if my career had taken another turn. But I have no regrets. Everything balances out.

The Great Depression fostered a generation of young people in New York City who knew what they were about because evidently their elders didn't. They had all the answers. Zeal was a measure of certainty. The Establishment represented the left-over stupidities of the last century. A good number who were concerned about the justice and dilemmas of the world were revolutionaries, although they didn't ape the Bolsheviks. They had their own shade of red. The ghost of John Reed hovered about. There was even a John Reed Club that held dances, socials, and esoteric lectures and discussions on Art and Society. The fiery speeches of Norman Thomas and Earl Browder and the cocksureness of their causes had some of the flavor of the romantic stories of the barricades of 1848 Paris.

There were benefit parties for unions in trouble. I remember Zero Mostel as the life of the party with his clown poker-face. There were also "pay the rent" parties, especially where a group of artists used the same loft. The Artists' Union was in the front lines.

One of its presidents, Paul Bloch, went off to Spain to join the Abraham Lincoln Brigade. He never came back.

The predominant intellectual milieu surrounding the Federal Art Project may have been somewhat as sketched above, but there were also many artists who were nonpolitical, who desperately wanted to pursue their careers, and who looked neither to the left or right. It was good to know your work went somewhere, gracing the walls of some public building. It gave you purpose and helped out a faltering self-esteem. It was not until years later you learned there was excess production and that, sadly, most of the work was eventually junked.

126
The Creative Printmakers Group is shown at work in 1939. The Group was created to introduce artists to the silkscreen process and to produce serigraph prints. Its clients included Saks Fifth Ave., Tiffany & Co., and the Metropolitan Museum of Art. From left: Constantine Velonis, unknown, Hyman Warsager, Thomas Quinn (President of the Artist's Union), Anthony Velonis.

This was not true of the poster division, however. Its work was requested by many public institutions and filled an immediate need without debate by the user as to what was good or bad art. I was hired by Mayor La Guardia's poster project of the Civilian Works Administration in 1934, when it was first organized by Audrey McMahon of the College Art Association. We began by painting single posters that were more like show cards, but quality quickly improved.

I was familiar with the silkscreening process and I thought it might be a useful adjunct to the poster division. John Weaver, the administrator, agreed, and in short order we were producing poster editions in the hundreds.

When the WPA Federal Art Project took over the CWA poster division, Richard Floethe was appointed administrator. He was an excellent designer, an expatriot graduate of the Bauhaus. He strove for the highest quality within the realistic potential of the artists there. There was a heavy influence from the work of Cassandre, the French poster artist. To design a poster that was satisfying to the customer and at the same time maintained artistic integrity was a challenge the poster artists met head on. It was easier with Richard Floethe on your side urging you to do your best.

When the silkscreen unit was on its feet technically, I went back to the designing section. At one point we were temporarily housed in a very large room. On the right wall was an unfinished mural. Every day Stuart Davis would mount a scaffold and paint away. After a while, I was not too surprised to find myself painting hard edges with colors right out of the tube. Jackson Pollock, Philip Evergood, Nahum Tchachasov, and many others I can't remember looked in on Stuart and talked shop.

Art philosophies were constantly argued, often quite passionately. One continuing controversy was "social significance" vs. "art for art's sake." Many, like myself, didn't follow either side. We felt that the individual artist was the best judge of his own work. Those who worked realistically or moderately stylized or impressionistically tended to "social significance," whereas the many abstract schools called their own work "visual music." Ad Reinhardt, Hananiah Harari, Eugene Morley and many others were advocates for abstraction. The others felt that not only should the themes comment on social problems, but that the work itself should be readily appreciated by the hoi polloi, the masses, the culturally impoverished.

This controversy reached a high point at a meeting held in the auditorium of the New School for Social Research. I remember the atmosphere hazily. The "Baroness" (some connection with Guggenheim) presented a series of large paintings by a German artist she thought was the greatest.* The paintings were more than abstract,

*The "Baroness" was Hilla Rebay (von Ehrenweisen) and the artist was Rudolf Bauer.

they were "nonobjective," all based on mathematical and geometric forms. Needless to say, the meeting was quite turbulent. The majority seemed to feel abstract art was arguable: it was human; it was play; it had occasional symbolism. But this nonobjective stuff had no content at all: it was cold and plodding. To this day, though, I can't see why it made so many artists angry. Many spoke up, but I remember the dashing, handsome figure of Byron Browne making an impassioned speech from the floor, after which half of the audience walked out. Informal panels continued to argue in the local coffee houses and cafeterias far into the night.

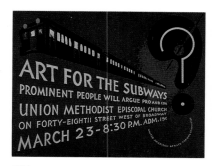

127
Anthony Velonis produced this poster after leaving the Federal Art Project. It advertised an unsuccessful project to provide art for New York subway stations.

The various art philosophies made their imprint on me. I had decided early that I would learn as much as I could from everybody. I felt the FAP was a golden opportunity. There had never been an art school as dynamic with so many crosscurrents.

There were undoubtedly in all the projects people who had no business being there. But they were a very small percentage. This was inevitable when the projects had to include without prejudice a wide spectrum of aesthetics. There were a few who "boondoggled," but not intentionally. I'm sure their ineptitude tortured them. I knew of one person whose work was always rejected. He became so discouraged that he quit and his family went back on "home relief."

As early as 1934 I was convinced that silkscreen, as an art medium, had a great potential, and I experimented toward that end. By 1936 I was messianic about it, especially because I felt I was in a good place for my vision to catch on. I made a small print, **Auto Motif**, on my own. (It's now in the Smithsonian.) I also did a print from a design by Richard Halls, my closest friend on the poster project. I used these to impress the administration that something should be done to encourage artists to learn about this versatile graphic medium.

As an individual, I couldn't get on the agenda. The Public Use of Arts Committee (PUAC) was an ad hoc lobby to make better use

■

of the products of the Federal Art Project. The Committee pressed for art in the subways [127], sculpture in the parks, and other ideas. After about eighteen months of talking, Audrey McMahon finally assigned me to the graphic art division where I was to lead a series of artists, one at a time, through the techniques of the new medium. We were to make editions of about twenty-five prints.

128
Anthony Velonis demonstrates the silk-screen process to an art class at Brooklyn's Thomas Jefferson High School, 1938.

The graphic art division was a fascinating place. There was Gus Peck, later on the Brooklyn Museum staff, polishing a hundred pound Bavarian litho stone. Eugene Morley was turning a classic hand press to squeeze out a color litho proof. Hyman Warsager was pulling large, color woodblock prints from a Franklin press. Harry Sternberg was having a good time with a monotype. Joseph LeBoit was printing an aquatint. The project director was Lynd Ward, the famous book illustrator who worked in woodcuts. Lynd was one of the gentlest and most understanding people I've ever met.

The first artist I worked with was Louis Lozowick. We turned out an interesting, rather stark composition of city rooftops. Harry Gottlieb and Elizabeth Olds did a print each. Ruth Chaney did a charming semi-abstract of a Greenwich Village street scene. Hyman Warsager did a textured treatment of a Coney Island beach. Eugene Morley did two prints, my favorites, each done in a different abstract style. I squeezed in a couple of my own prints.

Harry Shokler, Leonard Pytlak, and Bernard Steffens became enthusiastic with the new graphic medium and began to produce prints privately. Harry Shokler even wrote an instruction book about screen printing for artists.

Over the years screen printing has been evolving technically, especially in the manner of making the stencils. Today's photo-emulsion materials can do almost anything lithography can do. As a result, specialized printers can reproduce almost any painting with remarkable virtuosity and inventiveness. I had never thought of a reproduction as an original print. There is a distinction.

I tried to assess and use the limitations and special characteristics of the medium—without being a purist. The medium would be manipulated by the artist as he or she played with the colors—overlapping thin transparencies, or thick opaque laydown, etc. Even the stencil shapes might be changed radically in midstream. The sketch should be a guide only. Who ever heard of a woodblock as a means of reproducing a painting or a pencil sketch? The character of the wood, as the natural limit of the medium, produces its own beauty.

Working with other artists on the FAP in '38 and '39, I had accumulated an inventory of printerly possibilities to express in my own print. It turned out to be a tongue-in-cheek abstract still life I called **Decoration Empire** because some of the elements were reminiscent of Napoleonic pseudoclassicism. I used an extremely coarse screen with heavy impasto color; or I pushed paint through burlap and organdy; and at another stage, I used the finest mesh screen I could get to print soft gradations. In one printing I even softened them further by blotting wet color with newsprint. One could hardly call this "purist."

In the spring of 1939 the artists longest on the job received their "pink slips," myself included. I joined four other graphic artists to found "The Creative Printmakers Group" [126]. At first we struggled mostly with making our own prints. Then we screened small editions for other artists, whom we coached to make their own stencils directly on the silk. I remember Adolph Dehn and Federico Castellano. Later we screened many reproductions of Paul Klee for the Nierendorff Gallery. We did screened illustrations for limited edition books for Hyperion Press. We made special large Christmas cards for Saks, Tiffany, and the Metropolitan Museum of Art. The Met, through Ben Knotts, commissioned us to reproduce some of the Pennsylvania German art for the Index of American Design, from the precious originals made by WPA artists. This was a large loose-leaf folio.

Back to 1940: Carl Zigrosser, Director of the Weyhe Gallery, organized an exhibition of screen prints. In the catalog he put forth a new word: "serigraph." One day in March or April of 1938 I was in the great hall of the New York Public Library. I remember sifting through Greek and Latin roots for a suitable prefix to attach to "graphy," as in lithography, or "stonewriting."

I felt the fine art version needed a better word than "silkscreen process." "Seri," for silk, seemed suitable, thus, "serigraphy." I thought the word would have a better chance to take if a recognized print authority like Carl Zigrosser would introduce it at the exhibition [16] and in some of his writings. It took.

Once off the project, there was a subtle change in my status. I emerged with a modest standing in art and printmaking. Consequently, when Col. Brehon Somervell was appointed to phase out the projects, I was one of the "knowledgeable" artists invited by the Colonel to attend a special meeting concerning the future of the FAP. My impression is that about thirty artists attended. Somervell was quite cleverly ingenuous, feigning an openness that fooled no one. He said he had no choice but to cut down on the projects. The problem was, what standards should he use? It seemed to him that the best way was to dismiss according to relative merit. It was obvious that some artists were better than others and, he said, it was to the benefit of the projects and the taxpaying public that the best artists be retained the longest. The problem was that he knew what he liked, but that he was hardly an expert. He knew as much about art as the average plumber. Would some of the knowledgeable artists present constitute a committee to help him? This struck the artists as ridiculous, if not sadistic and cynical. They said, in effect, that they would not officiate in the dismissal of any fellow artist. There was some shouting as they filed out. This was predictable, but perhaps Somervell was playing a kind of poker. After the meeting he could claim that artists didn't want to help him, so then he had a free hand to do the job he had to do.

In retrospect, we can see that the WPA/FAP allowed artists to continue and advance with their work until the economy was able to absorb their special skills or the newer marketable skills (as in my case) that the habit of creativity engendered. Secretary of Labor, Frances Perkins and F.D.R. rescued a generation of artists to become productive citizens instead of cynical revolutionaries. Still, after all this time, the salvaging of human resources for useful work is a lesson we have not yet learned. In particular there should be another effect from this book. It's a lesson about integrity of product. In art, even more strikingly than in general commerce, the integrity of the producer is vital and should be encouraged by dealers, agents, and middlemen. In this case, feedback from the consumer tends to corrupt. It brings up a basic ethical problem. In effect, Richard Floethe told his clients: "You get strawberries and cream, or nothing." This attitude bred the high quality of poster art that his unit produced.

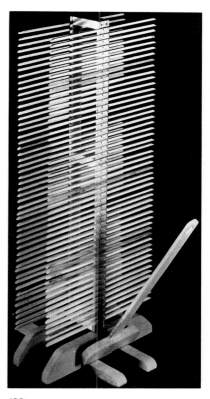

129
This print drying rack was designed and constructed by Velonis for use by the N.Y.C. poster division. It was later adapted for other printmaking and photographic processes.

130
Aida McKenzie
New York, NY
74 x 107 cm.
29 x 42 in.

U.S. Travel Bureau Posters

Under the New Deal, the U.S. Travel Bureau set out to awaken Americans' interest in their homeland. Given the conditions of the time—much of Europe and Asia were embroiled in war in the late 1930s—Americans' opportunities for travel abroad were severely limited and, in any case, the harsh economic realities faced by most U.S. citizens made distant travel a mere pipe dream.

The promotional campaign organized during the New Deal in some ways foreshadowed the **See America First** campaign promoted by the Johnson administration in the 1960s. WPA/FAP artists were engaged in creating travel posters for the bureau, which clearly reveal deep appreciation of the wonders of the diverse American landscape. In their choice of imagery, colors, composition, and type, these posters forcefully capture the grandeur of the vistas of the Southwest, the unique flavor of the Amish and Mennonite communities still alive in Pennsylvania, and the vastness of Montana's rugged mountains.

These images encapsulate a strong theme that underlies many of the WPA posters: In showing a landscape of ferocious proportions and physical challenge, the posters reaffirmed and exulted in America as a place of opportunity and personal advancement. They explicitly urged, "See America," but they also asked that we re-see America as a land capable of providing sustenance and a rebirth of spirit. This spirit was a resource the nation badly needed in its struggle during trying economic circumstance.

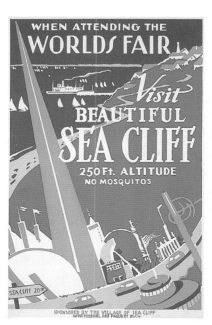

131
Artist unknown
New York, NY
56 x 36 cm.
22 x 14 in.

132
Jerome Roth
(Rothstein)
New York, NY
71 x 56 cm.
28 x 22 in.

133
Frank S. Nicholson
New York, NY
71 x 56 cm.
28 x 22 in.

134
Richard Halls
New York, NY
71 x 56 cm.
28 x 22 in.

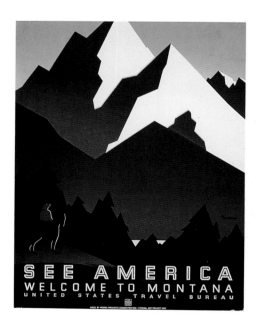

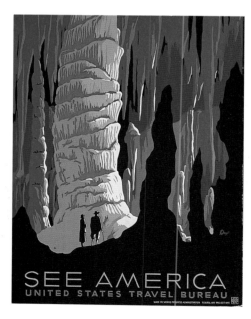

135
Martin Weitzman
New York, NY
71 x 56 cm.
28 x 22 in.

136
Alexander Dux
New York, NY
71 x 56 cm.
28 x 22 in.

137
Harry Herzog
New York, NY
71 x 56 cm.
28 x 22 in.

138
Robert Muchley
Philadelphia, PA
64 x 48 cm.
25 x 19 in.
Woodblock

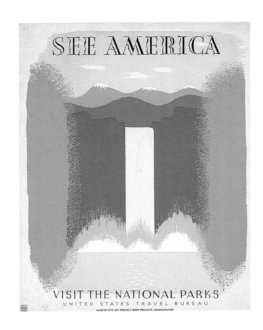

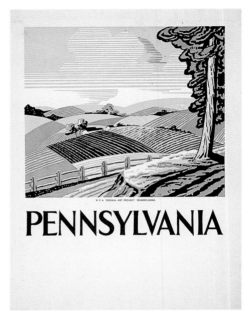

The poster division in Pennsylvania
experimented with printing methods
other than silkscreen. Posters 138–140
were produced as woodcuts.

139
Robert Muchley
Philadelphia, PA
64 x 48 cm.
25 x 19 in.
Woodblock

140
Isadore Posoff
Philadelphia, PA
63 x 45 cm.
25 x 17¾ in.
Woodblock

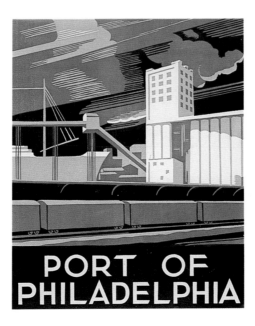

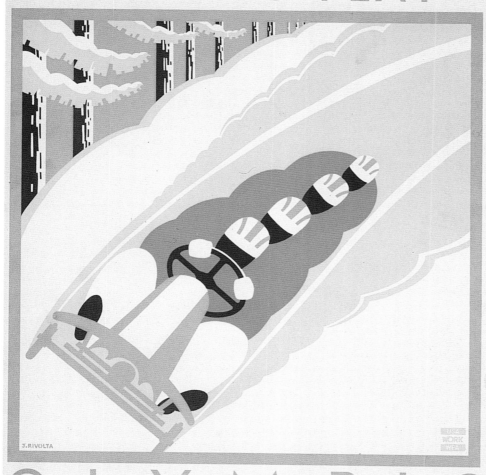

141
Jack Rivolta
New York, NY
63 x 42 cm.
25 x 16½ in.

142
Harry Herzog
New York, NY
71 x 56 cm.
28 x 22 in.

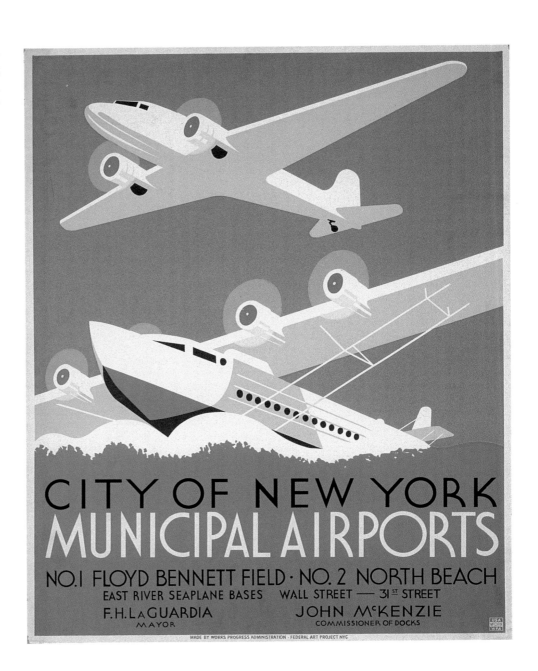

Education and Civic Activity Posters

Education was an important goal of the New Deal social planners. Numerous federal programs created to meet this goal included programs offering remedial education, job training, and career guidance. The activities of the National Youth Association (NYA) stand as prime examples of the educational opportunities fostered by the New Deal.

At its peak, the NYA had monthly enrollments of some 200,000 young people. It furnished educational stipends for college students and provided jobs in libraries, museums, and laboratories. (For instance, Duke University law student Richard Nixon received 35 cents an hour for his work in the law library.) Programs for apprentice training in many occupations—furniture making, butchering, and welding among them—were also administered by the NYA.

Inexpensively produced in large quantities, powerfully communicative with strong graphic designs and imagery, the posters created by the artists of the WPA/FAP proved an important and effective medium for informing the public about the various opportunities made available to them by the NYA and similar agencies. Other educational venues that the posters promoted included the WPA-run Workers Education Program, designed to encourage adult education, and the Women's and Professional Division, which provided training in home economics and health care. Public lectures also provided for the dissemination of information dealing with such topics as parenting, scientific research advances, the environment, and current events. These educational opportunities were publicized with posters created by the FAP.

143
Artist unknown
New York, NY
56 x 36 cm.
22 x 14 in.

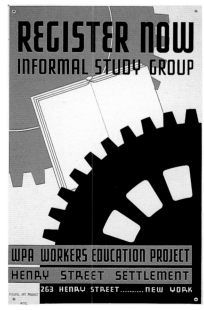

144
Artist unknown
New York, NY
56 x 36 cm.
22 x 14 in.

145
Albert M. Bender
Chicago, IL
56 x 36 cm.
22 x 14 in.

146
Albert M. Bender
Chicago, IL
56 x 36 cm.
22 x 14 in.

147
Samuel Brown and
Morris Katz
Cleveland, OH
71 x 56 cm.
28 x 22 in.

148
Harry Herzog
New York, NY
56 x 36 cm.
22 x 14 in.

■

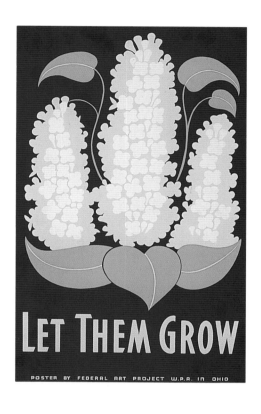

149
Stanley T. Clough
Cleveland, OH
56 x 36 cm.
22 x 14 in.

150
Stanley T. Clough
Cleveland, OH
56 x 36 cm.
22 x 14 in.

151
Beard
Chicago, IL
56 x 36 cm.
22 x 14 in.

152
Beard
Chicago, IL
56 x 36 cm.
22 x 14 in.

153
Albert M. Bender
Chicago, IL
56 x 36 cm.
22 x 14 in.

■

154
Albert M. Bender
Chicago, IL
56 x 36 cm.
22 x 14 in.

Albert Bender is represented by enthusiastic and energetic designs that he produced for the Chicago bureau of the WPA. These posters and figures 145, 146 show skillful handling of the human form and excellent understanding of typography.

155
R.E.K. (signed)
Chicago, IL
56 x 36 cm.
22 x 14 in.

156
Erel Osborn
Chicago, IL
56 x 36 cm.
22 x 14 in.

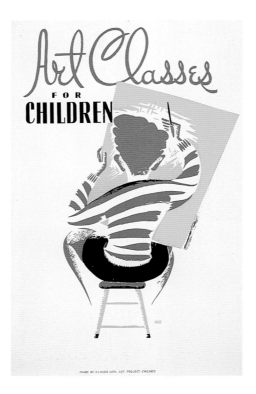

157
Artist unknown
Chicago, IL
56 x 36 cm.
22 x 14 in.

158
Ned B. Schnellock
New York, NY
56 x 36 cm.
22 x 14 in.

159
Cleo Sara
Chicago, IL
56 x 36 cm.
22 x 14 in.

160
Arlington Gregg
Chicago, IL
56 x 36 cm.
22 x 14 in.

The importance and pleasure of books is joyously communicated in these designs by Chicago artists for the public library system.

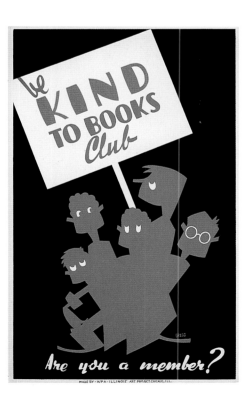

161
Albert M. Bender
(attributed)
Chicago, IL
56 x 36 cm.
22 x 14 in.

162
Arlington Gregg
Chicago, IL
56 x 36 cm.
22 x 14 in.

163
John Buczak
Chicago, IL
56 x 36 cm.
22 x 14 in.

■

164
Beard
Chicago, IL
56 x 36 cm.
22 x 14 in.

The nighttime wonders of America's "Second City" are pictured in this pair of posters. The spray of illuminated water from the Buckingham Fountain was created by the direct application of tusche crayon to the printing screen.

165
Hugh Stevenson
Philadelphia, PA
64 x 48 cm.
25 x 19 in.
Woodblock

166
Frank Weathers Long
Chicago, IL
56 x 36 cm.
22 x 14 in.

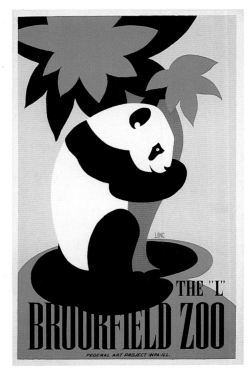

167
Arlington Gregg
Chicago, IL
56 x 36 cm.
22 x 14 in.

168
Arlington Gregg
Chicago, IL
56 x 36 cm.
22 x 14 in.

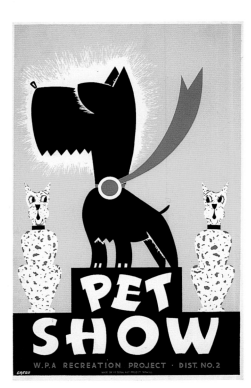

169
Carken
Chicago, IL
35 x 56 cm.
14 x 22 in.

The need for wildlife conservation is underscored subtly in two posters [170, 171] created for the National Park Service. Note the transparent quality of the headlights and the sunlight.

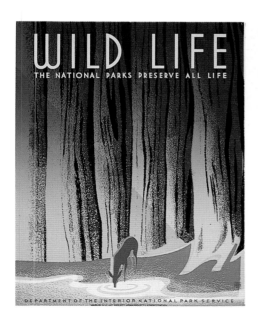

170
Frank S. Nicholson
(attributed)
New York, NY
71 x 56 cm.
28 x 22 in.

171
John Wagner
New York, NY
71 x 56 cm.
28 x 22 in.

■

172
D.S. (signed)
Chicago, IL
71 x 51 cm.
28 x 20 in.

Each of these posters combines distinctive type treatments with abstract and Cubist-influenced pictoral elements. These designs predate images more widely seen in the 1950s.

■

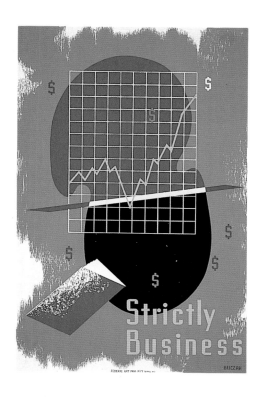

173
John Buczak
Chicago, IL
76 x 51 cm.
30 x 20 in.

174
Galic
Chicago, IL
56 x 36 cm.
22 x 14 in.

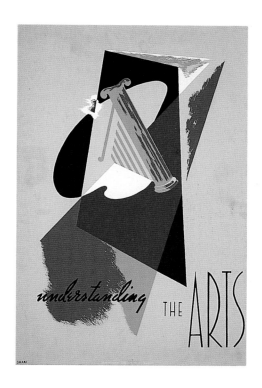

175
Shari Weisberg
Chicago, IL
76 x 51 cm.
30 x 20 in.

176
Shari Weisberg
Chicago, IL
76 x 51 cm.
30 x 20 in.

177
Vera Bock
New York, NY
71 x 46 cm.
28 x 18 in.

178
Vera Bock
New York, NY
71 x 46 cm.
28 x 18 in.

179
Vera Bock
New York, NY
71 x 46 cm.
28 x 18 in.

180
Vera Bock
New York, NY
71 x 46 cm.
28 x 18 in.

181
Vera Bock
New York, NY
71 x 46 cm.
28 x 18 in.

The distinctive mock-woodcut style
that Vera Bock achieved with silkscreen
is shown here. Each of these posters,
incorporating blocks of type within the
illustration, reveals her training as a
book illustrator.

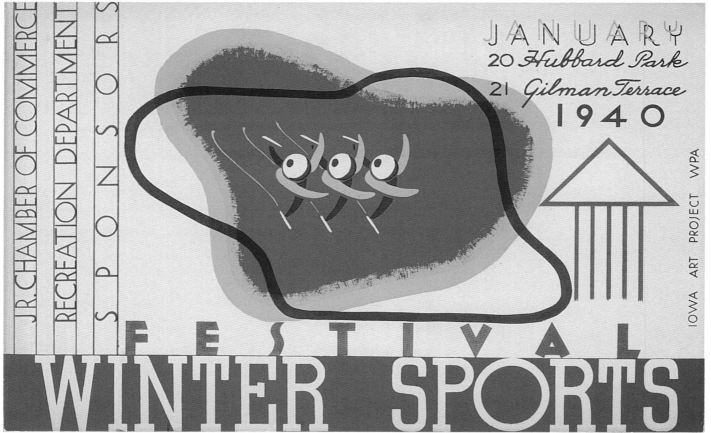

182
Artist unknown
Sioux City, IA
36 x 56 cm.
14 x 22 in.

183
Kreger
Chicago, IL
76 x 51 cm.
30 x 20 in.

184
Estelle Levine
New York, NY
71 x 56 cm.
28 x 22 in.

185
Charles Verschuuren
New York, NY
70 x 55 cm.
27½ x 21½ in.

186
Kenneth Whitley
Chicago, IL
76 x 51 cm.
30 x 20 in.

■

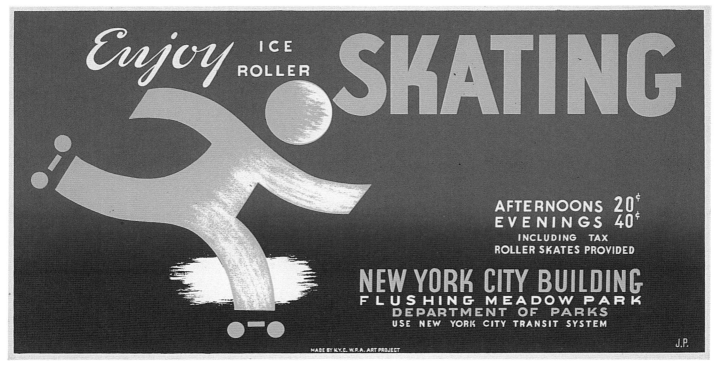

187
J.P. (signed)
New York, NY
28 x 53 cm.
11 x 21 in.

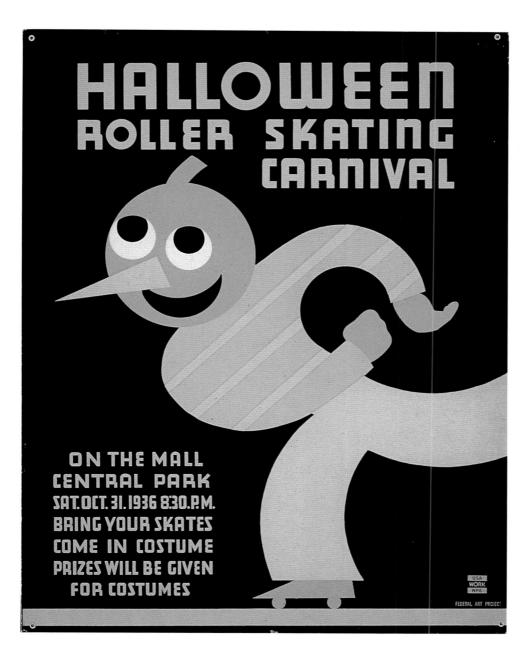

188
Artist unknown
New York, NY
71 x 56 cm.
28 x 22 in.

189
Merlin
Detroit, MI
71 x 56 cm.
28 x 22 in.

190
Blanche L. Anish
Cincinnati, OH
70 x 55 cm.
27½ x 21½ in.

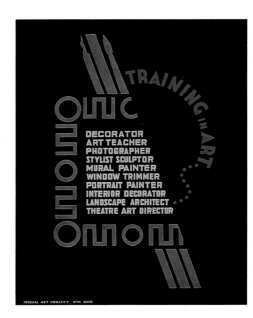

191
Harry Herzog
New York, NY
71 x 56 cm.
28 x 22 in.

192
Artist unknown
Iowa
56 x 36 cm.
22 x 14 in.

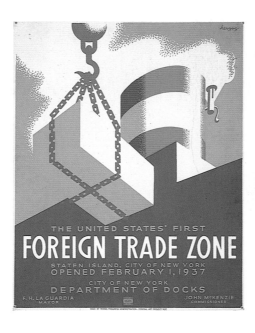

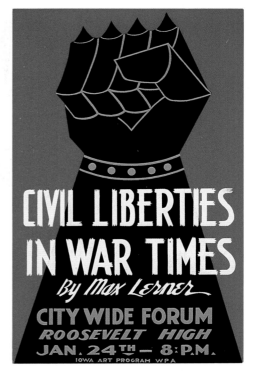

193
Martin Weitzman
New York, NY
71 x 56 cm.
28 x 22 in.

Each of these works shows the importance
of good typography in the design of a
successful poster.

A Design Perspective
by Jim Heimann

The posters created for the Works Progress Administration's Federal Art Project display influences from many modern art movements that began in Europe during the first forty years of this century. But the WPA poster artists, breaking away from their country's limited art traditions, often achieved something more than mere derivation. In absorbing, redefining, and applying these contemporary European styles to the needs of the poster units, the WPA artists developed a fresh style that was uniquely American.

The modern-age catalyst for many American artists was the shocking Armory Show of 1913, which exposed in one bold stroke all that was important in contemporary European art. Exhibited in New York and Chicago, the Armory Show ignored the representational tenets and Beaux Arts tradition that were the mainstay of American art. Instead it embraced the progressive, disturbing ideas pervasive in the art capitals of Europe, introducing the concepts of Fauvism, Cubism, Futurism, Dada, Surrealism, the Bauhaus, and other avant-garde movements to follow.

Several factors contributed to the successful integration of these modern movements in American graphic arts. For one thing, advertising was increasingly influential and helped to develop mass-communication arts. The new professions of graphic designer, illustrator, and commercial artist received substantial validation with the establishment in 1920 of the influential Art Directors Club of New York. The propaganda surrounding World War I had initiated mass communication on a global level, which combined with postwar prosperity and new technology, led to the maturation of the commercial arts in the United States.

In addition, European art periodicals, such as the influen-

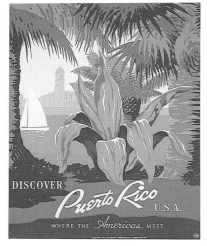

194
Frank S. Nicholson
New York, NY
71 x 56 cm.
28 x 22 in.

tial German magazines **Das Plakate** and **Gebrauchsgraphik**, were becoming available to American artists, exposing them to design, illustration, typography, and photography outside the context of fine art. Americans also received lessons in how to assimilate the European modernist experience from the immigrants who relocated in the United States during the Depression. These included Bauhaus expatriates Laszlo Moholy-Nagy, Walter Gropius, and Herbert Bayer, who provided a direct link to the European art revolution, and Dr. Mehemed Fehmy Agha at **Vogue** and Alexy Brodovich at **Harper's Bazaar**, art directors who applied forward-thinking graphic designs to popular American content.

By the 1930s, the stylistic experimentation of Europe during the previous two decades had provided Americans with an artistic foundation from which to assert a viewpoint typically American. Artists reacted to the deteriorating social conditions of the deepening Depression by strongly addressing socio-political issues in their art. Alternatively, the growing spirit of regionalism, or the so-called American Scene style practiced by such artists as Grant Wood and Thomas Hart Benton, represented at once a retreat to the agrarian background of America and a repudiation of the highly intellectualized, sometimes esoteric, European "-isms."

These influences were evident when the WPA / FAP poster program was formed. The artists who were hired to work in the poster units arrived with varied dispositions and styles and, under the loose guidelines of the FAP, put their diversity to use in dramatic ways. Poster unit directors encouraged experimentation, which was liberating. One important concern in the choice of styles and designs was the reproduction method used. The silkscreen process was well suited to the requirement that the bold, eye-catching posters communicate quickly. Stylization and simplicity were inherent properties of the process, but allowed little latitude in pictorial representation. Naturalism could be accom-

195
Jack Rivolta
New York, NY
71 x 56 cm,
28 x 22 in.

196
Artist unknown
Chicago, IL
76 x 51 cm.
30 x 20 in.

■

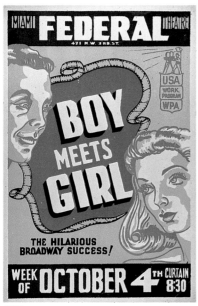

197
Artist unknown
Location unknown
56 x 36 cm.
22 x 14 in.

198
Artist unknown
Iowa
56 x 36 cm.
22 x 14 in.

plished by using techniques such as stylized shadows, fade-away stippling, and the reduction of images to their geometrical simplicity. As the poster artists gained experience and mastered the silkscreen process, they expressed design confidence. In their work, the visual legacy amassed during the previous thirty years emerged fully articulated.

Many of the posters used an asymmetrical format, a placement that was thought to create tension and disturb the viewer's complacency, thus emphasizing the message [198]. Where type was the sole design element, however, symmetry tended to dominate the composition [30, 57]. Humor, a vital element in many of the posters, shows up in the whimsical **Funny Side Up** character [199], who suggests a lighthearted mood reminiscent of stylized 1920s print cartoons popularized by the work of John Held, Jr. The more commercial-looking posters reveal the training of the show-card artist [197]. The influence of the European poster masters was not overlooked: A.M. Cassandre's **Normandie** and **L'Atlantique** posters, for example, clearly inspired **Foreign Trade Zone** [6]; and **Winter in N.Y. State** [195] owes its imagery to the stylized travel posters of Joseph Binder and the magazine covers of Edouardo Benito.

Elsewhere, influences of the various modern art movements are evident, such as the Surrealist's stylized eye [32, 38, 176]. The Cubists' and Constructivists' experiments with collage—adapting type, torn paper, multiple layers and overlaying, which created a dimensional effect—appeared in many posters [48, 49, 50, 68, 196]. Even when attempting designs with more traditional and figurative imagery, the WPA artists produced successes. In the "See America" series [132-136] and in **Discover Puerto Rico** [194], the abbreviated elements are easily bridged by rich color and shading, alluding to a naturalistic style. Conversely, a highly abstracted and symbolic style [174, 175] may have stretched public perception of the modern aesthetic, or been rejected outright as undecipherable.

Taken as an aggregate, the posters display a skilled application and synthesis of modern fine art and commercial art principles of the first four decades of the twentieth century. In addition to providing a public service, the posters exposed the public to sophisticated art applied to the commonplace. Their iconography paved the way for public acceptance of abstract art, as imagery created in the 1930s was eventually absorbed on a popular level in the 1950s. Ultimately, the art of the WPA can be measured by its continued influence and these rediscovered posters evaluated by their still-fresh aesthetics fifty years after they were created.

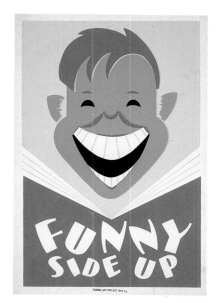

199
Albert M. Bender
(attributed)
Chicago, IL
76 x 51 cm.
30 x 20 in.

Jim Heimann is a graphic designer and author. He is a faculty member of the Otis/Parsons School of Design, Los Angeles, and has lectured extensively on graphic design and American roadside vernacular architecture.

200
Artist unknown
Cleveland, OH
71 x 48 cm.
28 x 19 in.

The influence of American designer Otis
Shepard is apparent in the graphic planes
of the broadly smiling figure. Note the
mezzotint effect in the sweater.

MILK
FOR SUMMER THIRST
CLEVELAND DIVISION OF HEALTH · FOOD AND DRUG ADMINISTRATION '40

Health and Safety Posters

During his second inaugural address in 1936, Franklin Roosevelt issued his famous statement that he unhappily still saw "one-third of a nation ill-housed, ill-clad and ill-nourished." The president's observation reiterated the New Deal's commitment to curing some of the major social problems facing the country.

One method used to attack these problems was the creation of health posters to inform citizens of agencies and services available to them. These health posters had an immediate bearing on the quality of life. Unfit housing, cancer, nutrition, and personal hygiene were just some of the social ills and medical issues addressed in these artworks. An important factor in the posters' effectiveness was their nonjudgmental tone, for they were intended, not to frighten or shame, but to present information directing the reader toward an effective course of action.

This nonjudgmental tone was particularly important as poster artists attacked the critical but sensitive problem of venereal disease. Longtime social taboos against public discussion of sexually transmitted disease were broken down as the posters urged the public to seek treatment unashamedly. Another issue addressed in the posters was safety in the workplace. Careful work procedures were stressed in hopes of reducing the number of job-related accidents. Warnings such as "Protect Your Hands" and "Work With Care" provided direct and important messages to the nation's workers in colorful, eye-catching graphics.

201
Artist Unknown
Cleveland, OH
71 x 48 cm.
28 x 19 in.

202
Charles Verschuuren
New York, NY
56 x 36 cm.
22 x 14 in.

203
Artist unknown
Chicago, IL
56 x 36 cm.
22 x 14 in.

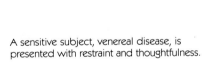

A sensitive subject, venereal disease, is
presented with restraint and thoughtfulness.

204
Artist unknown
Chicago, IL
56 x 36 cm.
22 x 14 in.

205
Artist unknown
Chicago, IL
56 x 36 cm.
22 x 14 in.

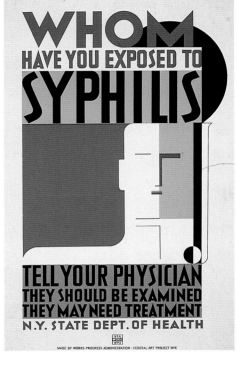

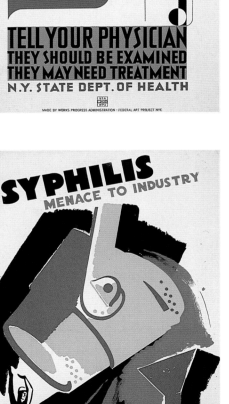

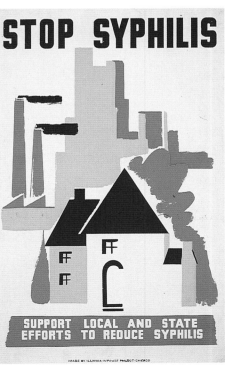

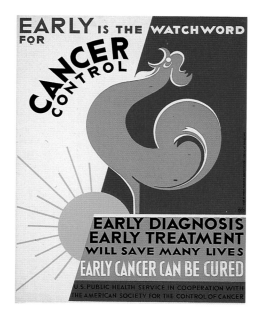

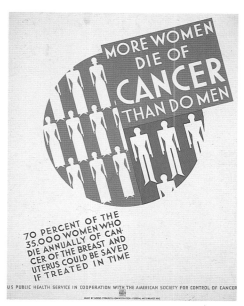

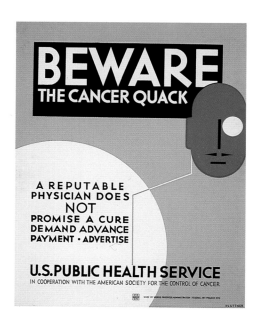

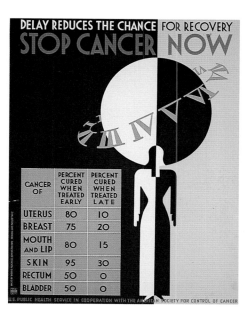

206
Charles Verschuuren
New York, NY
71 x 56 cm.
28 x 22 in.

207
Alex Kallenberg
New York, NY
71 x 56 cm.
28 x 22 in.

In the 1930s the discussion of cancer was a social taboo. These posters helped break down barriers that prevented public dissemination of information.

208
Max Plattner
New York, NY
71 x 56 cm.
28 x 22 in.

209
Artist unknown
New York, NY
71 x 56 cm.
28 x 22 in.

210
Robert Muchley
Philadelphia, PA
64 x 48 cm.
25 x 19 in.
Woodblock

During a decade in which the rights of
workers was a major social concern, these
posters directly addressed health and
safety issues important to all workers.

WPA FEDERAL ART PROJECT PENNSYLVANIA

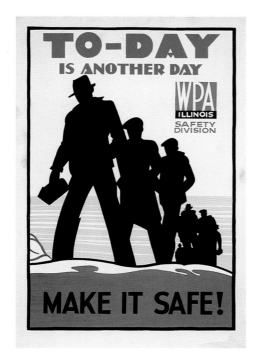

211
Artist unknown
Chicago, IL
76 x 51 cm.
30 x 20 in.
Preliminary design
mixed medium

212
John Mathews
Chicago, IL
76 x 51 cm.
30 x 20 in.
Preliminary design
mixed medium

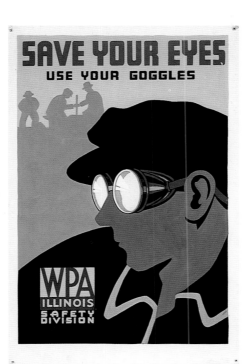

213
Robert Muchley
Philadelphia, PA
51 x 41 cm.
20 x 16 in.
Lithograph

214
Artist unknown
Chicago, IL
76 x 51 cm.
30 x 20 in.
Preliminary design
mixed medium

■

215
Artist unknown
Rochester, NY
56 x 36 cm.
22 x 14 in.

216
Artist Unknown
Rochester, NY
56 x 36 cm.
22 x 14 in.

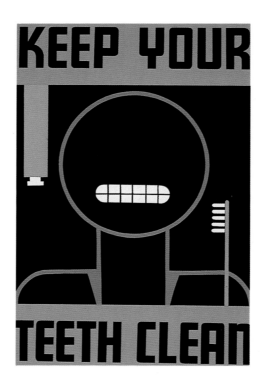

217
Foster Humfreville
and Alex Kallenberg
New York, NY
71 x 56 cm.
28 x 22 in.

218
Charles Verschuuren
New York, NY
56 x 36 cm.
22 x 14 in.

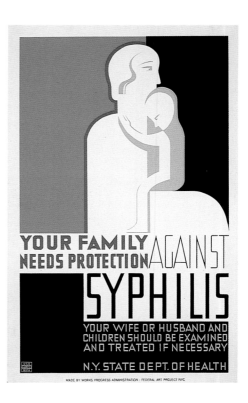

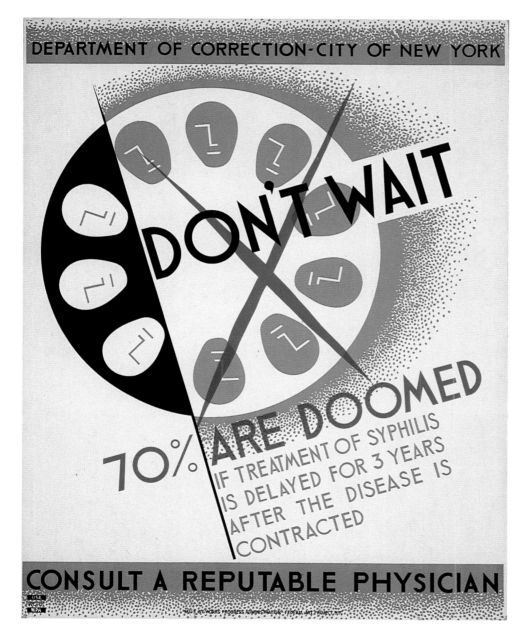

219
Artist unknown
New York, NY
71 x 56 cm.
28 x 22 in.

The anti-syphilis posters shown here present a forthright approach to the eradication of venereal disease. They confront the viewer with their message and urge action.

220
Walter C. Pettee
New York, NY
71 x 56 cm.
28 x 22 in.

221
Herman Kessler
(attributed)
New York, NY
71 x 56 cm.
28 x 22 in.

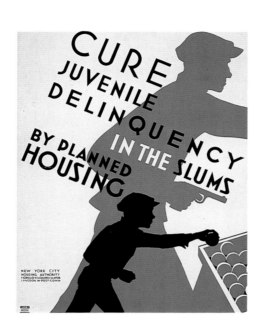

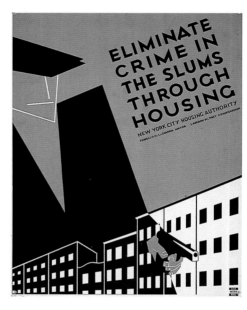

A priority for New Deal social planners
was low-cost public housing, which these
posters promote and celebrate.

222
John Wagner
New York, NY
71 x 56 cm.
28 x 22 in.

223
Muller
New York, NY
56 x 36 cm.

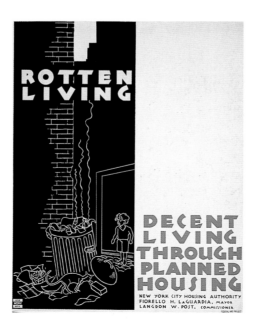

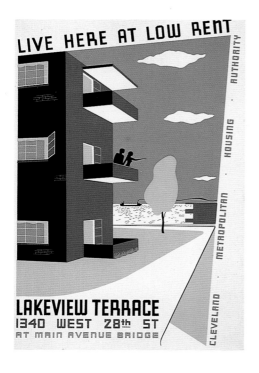

224
Stanley T. Clough
Cleveland, OH
71 x 48 cm.
28 x 19 in.

225
Artist unknown
Cleveland, OH
71 x 48 cm.
28 x 19 in.

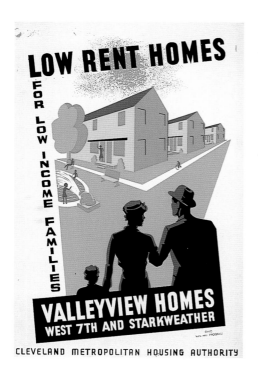

226
Artist unknown
Cleveland, OH
71 x 48 cm.
28 x 19 in.

227
Estelle Levine
New York, NY
71 x 56 cm.
28 x 22 in.

228
Ben Kaplan
New York, NY
56 x 36 cm.
22 x 14 in.

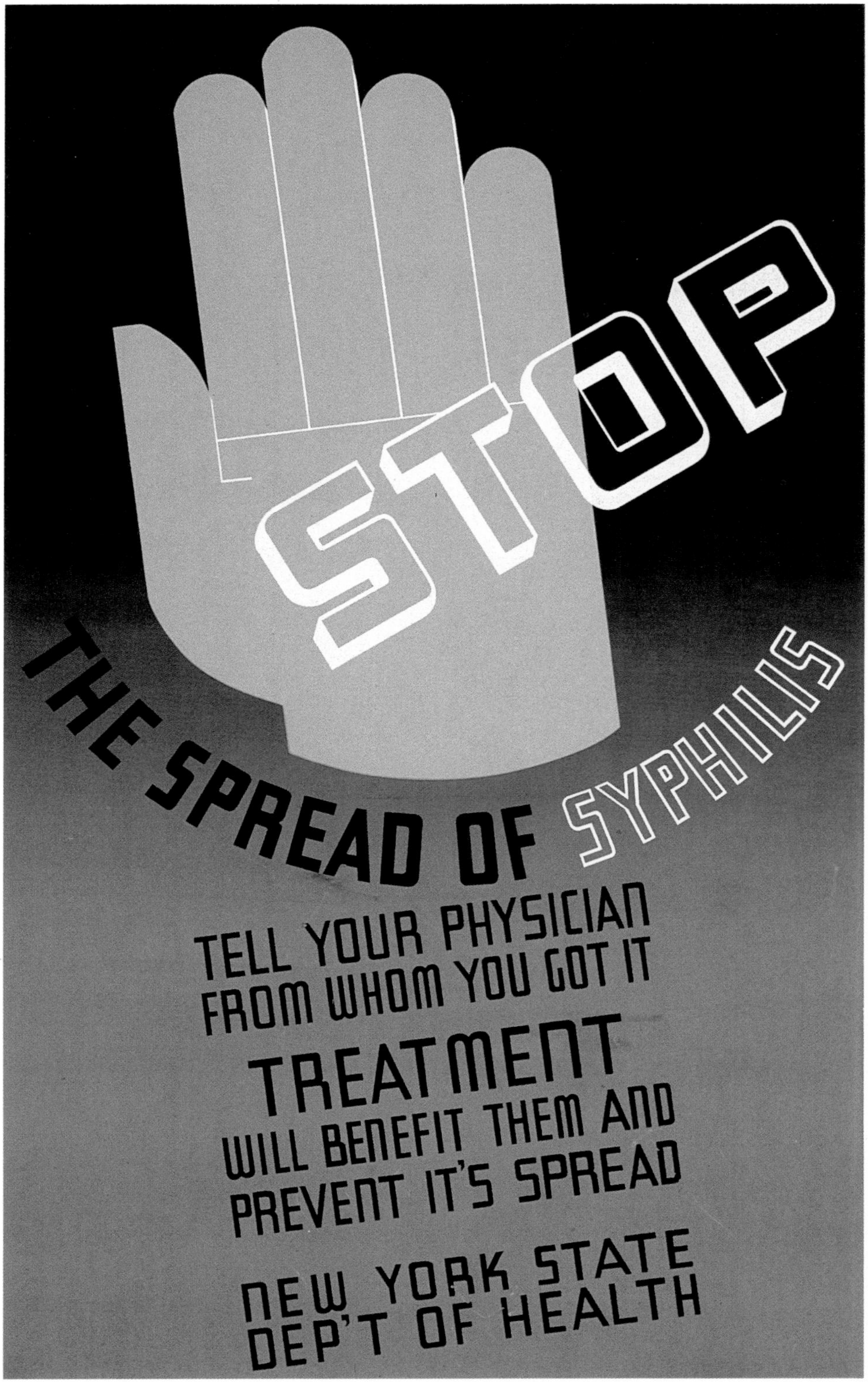

The split-font background adds depth to this forceful anti-venereal disease poster.

■

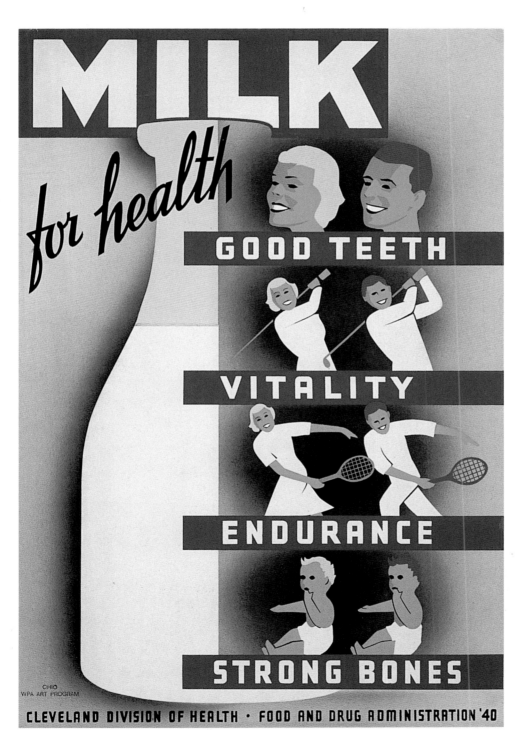

229
Artist unknown
Cleveland, OH
71 x 48 cm.
28 x 19 in.

This poster combines airbrush with silk-screen techniques.

230
Artist unknown
Chicago, IL
56 x 36 cm.
22 x 14 in.

The textural potential of the silkscreen process is successfully utilized in this fire prevention poster.

■

231
Nathan Sherman
Philadelphia, PA
65 x 48 cm.
25½ x 19 in.
Lithograph

232
Earl Schuler
Cleveland, OH
71 x 56 cm.
28 x 22 in.

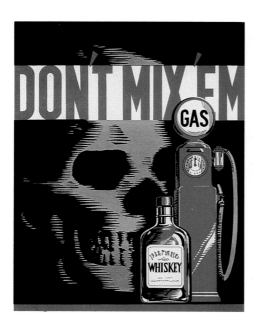

233
Robert Lachenmann
Philadelphia, PA
47 x 37 cm.
18½ x 14½ in.
Woodblock

234
Vera Bock
New York, NY
56 x 36 cm.
22 x 14 in.

235
Allan Nase
Philadelphia, PA
54 x 44 cm.
21¼ x 17¼ in.
Lithograph

WPA FEDERAL ART PROJECT PENNSYLVANIA

236
Nathan Sherman
Philadelphia, PA
61 x 46 cm.
Woodblock

A Remembrance of the WPA Poster Division
by Richard Floethe

SELF PORTRAIT
Richard Floethe

Artist's Portrait Prints
·· THE SIXTH OF THE SERIES ··
to be shown through November 1935

237
Self-portrait, circa 1935.

New York in 1936 was a safe city. There was no parking problem. The subway was five cents, the buses ten cents, drinks cost twenty-five cents, and one could eat well at one dollar. My studio was in Chelsea (West 20th Street) and my rent was $55.00 a month. It was at this place that my telephone rang periodically at eight a.m. and somebody on the line would ask for Morris of the laundry and every time the eight o'clock call came on, I would answer "This is not Morris and this is not a laundry" and would hang up. It was a morning in May when the phone rang and as usual I answered "This is not Morris," and I was just ready to hang up when a voice asked for Mr. Floethe. The gentleman on the other end was Mr. Mortimer Kaufman, who explained his call. He said I had been recommended as a possible head of the poster division of the Federal Art Project. I was a freelance artist at this time (working on book illustrations and book design) and I was not too anxious to give up my independence. However, the offer intrigued me. I made an appointment with Mrs. Audrey McMahon and I was hired with an understanding that I would not have to keep strict office hours.

My assistant, my good man Friday, was Fred Bechter, a non-artist. My secretary, Nell de Coursey, had a reputation as being difficult. However, she turned out to be a gem, not difficult at all and very competent.

The staff of the poster division consisted mostly of young artists, some with experience and some just out of art school. I also inherited the silkscreen printing department. The poster division was in one place, the silkscreening department in another, and the administrative staff in yet another place. After about a year, most of the art projects were combined under one roof.

I had a dependable group of artists who produced consistently good work. There was Richard Halls, Jerry Rothstein, Vera Bock, Tony Velonis, Harry Herzog, Aida McKenzie, Bryan Burroughs, and half a dozen more. There was Ben Kaplan who was excellent at layout and lettering. Tony Velonis periodically disappeared to the graphic art division where he experimented in silkscreen processes.

The head of my silkscreen printing shop was Louis Schafrank. Louis was a great worrier and this sometimes caused friction in his department, but he ran it well and always met the deadlines.

We had one staffing problem. The Home Relief would send us artists and people who claimed to be artists. Most of them were unacceptable for my department, but we could not get rid of them. So I had a bright idea—I created a film-cutting department, which absorbed the inexperienced, and most of them became good film cutters.

I ran the department by posting incoming jobs on the bulletin board. Each artist made a series of small sketches. I would select one and let that artist proceed to make a rendering to scale. I would collect the best of the lot and send them to the customer. The one chosen by the customer would be developed in the finished art. This went to the film-cutting department for color separations and then into the print shop for printing.

Poster artists were not permitted to sign their work. I tried to change that but always ran into a stone wall. Maybe Washington bureaucrats considered posters as non-art.

Before coming to the United States in 1928 I had studied in Germany, my home. I was a roving art student: I picked the art schools for the instructors. Maybe one school had a fine graphics department, another was well known for painting and so on. I ended up at the Bauhaus because I became intrigued with their revolutionary approach to art and the function of the artist using his talents for creating beauty in the design of common objects. And I learned the possibilities and limitations of designing for mass production. Unfortunately, I only was able to spend one year at Weimar because of the rapidly falling mark and the inflation. However, this one year at the Bauhaus influenced my work permanently.

The poster division had plenty of work. We made posters for all governmental offices and tax-supported institutions. Occasionally, some politician tried to force his daughter's or son's designs down our throat, but such efforts were not successful. Hard cases were squashed by Mrs. McMahon. Audrey McMahon was a good administrator because she rarely interfered with the work of the department heads. Generally, the atmosphere among the departments was cordial. There was Lloyd Rollins of the easel division, Burgoyne Diller in the murals division, Gustav von Groschwitz (and later Lynd Ward) in the graphic art division, and Robert Godsoe, head of the exhibition division. The Index of American Design also did excellent work. The Allocation Committee was where all works from easel, murals, and graphic art were checked for quality and allocated. There was a grievance committee which had to listen to artists whose work had been found wanting.

In 1938 Mrs. McMahon conceived the idea of having a calendar made and distributing it to congressmen, senators, and members of the administration. The poster division was to design and print it. The idea was to make friends and supporters for the Federal Art Project. The result was not what we had expected. A congressman rose in the House waiving our gift calendar and accused the Art Project of squandering taxpayers' money. There followed what I would describe as a "stink." There were threats that heads would be rolling. But eventually it blew over. I am sure the congressman threw the calendar into the garbage. Had he held on to it he would be richer by $1,000, the price that was recently paid for the calendar [316].

238
Richard Floethe's design is featured prominently at this 1938 poster exhibition.

The exhibitions of our posters were rarely mentioned in the press. The only publications that reproduced our work were **Signs of the Times** and **Fortune**. Both magazines wrote complimentary articles about them.

I had married in 1937. My wife Louise and I bought a small farm in Orange County, New York. We worked over weekends to make it livable since we intended to make it our permanent home. The increase of work in the poster department began to take too much of my time and my private commitments suffered (I was working on book illustrations). By 1939 I felt it was time to leave the project.

The announcement of my leaving raised the suspicion among my artists that I had been fired. Tony Velonis and Richard Halls were ready to start a demonstration on my behalf. It took some convincing on my part to assure them that leaving was my decision.

It is now almost a half-century since I worked at the project and I still think with nostalgia of the wonderful experience I had working with an enthusiastic and talented group of artists.

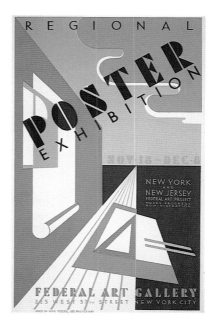

239
Richard Floethe
New York, NY
56 x 36 cm.
22 x 14 in.

■

240
Bryan Burroughs
New York, NY
56 x 36 cm.
22 x 14 in.

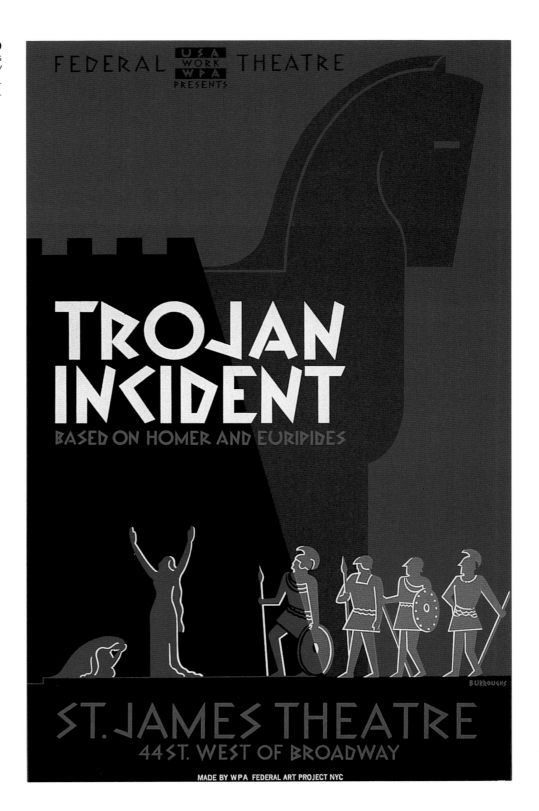

Federal Music Project and Federal Dance Project Posters

The Federal Music Project (FMP) began in 1935 as a division of the Federal Theatre Project. Headed by Nikolai Sokoloff, former director of the Cleveland Orchestra, the FMP strove to bring the great gifts of music to communities throughout America. It sponsored tens of thousands of performances of symphonic and popular works, offered music classes to the public in community centers across the nation, and presented the work of contemporary composers such as Ernst Bacon, Felix Borowski, A. Lehman Engel, Paul Bowles, Frederic Hart, and Robert Miles Delaney.

By 1939 the music project was providing employment for more than 7,000 musicians in 28 symphony orchestras, 55 dance bands, 15 chamber ensembles and 33 opera and choral units. In the four years of its existence the FMP groups gave 225,000 performances before audiences totaling more than 150 million people.

Equally dedicated to making the performance arts accessible to the public were the members of the Federal Dance Project (FDP), whose existence as a separate entity was short—from January 1936 to October 1937—before it was absorbed into the FTP. The FDP championed the new, radical art form of modern dance, much of it rich with social content. Its traveling troupes of dancers exposed citizens across the nation to the joys of movement set to music.

The FDP made great strides in increasing the repertoire of and expanding the audience for modern dance in America. Its pivotal figure was dancer Helen Tamiris, who had lobbied strongly for a federally-sponsored program; other FDP talents included choreographers Doris Humphrey and Charles Weidman (both considered among the pioneers of modern dance in America, along with Martha Graham) and then-dancers Bella Lewitsky and José Limón.

241
Bryan Burroughs
New York, NY
56 x 36 cm.
22 x 14 in.

242
Artist unknown
New York, NY
56 x 36 cm.
22 x 14 in.

243
Ben Lassen
New York, NY
56 x 36 cm.
22 x 14 in.

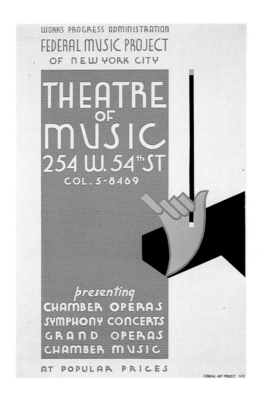

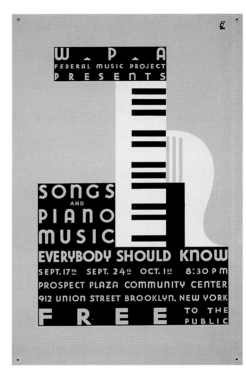

244
Ralph Graham
Chicago, IL
56 x 36 cm.
22 x 14 in.

245
Artist unknown
New York, NY
56 x 36 cm.
22 x 14 in.

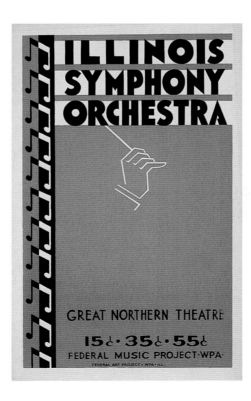

246
Carken
Chicago, IL
56 x 36 cm.
22 x 14 in.

This poster recalls an earlier, less enlightened era in America when "separate but equal" was still the rule.

247
Artist unknown
Sioux City, IA
56 x 36 cm.
22 x 14 in.

Particularly interesting is the drop shadow
effect in this excellent example of skillfully
hand-cut type.

■

248
Artist unknown
New York, NY
56 x 36 cm.
22 x 14 in.

249
Martin Weitzman
New York, NY
56 x 36 cm.
22 x 14 in.

250
Richard Halls
New York, NY
56 x 36 cm.
22 x 14 in.

251
Artist unknown
New York, NY
56 x 36 cm.
22 x 14 in.

252
Ben Sheer
New York, NY
28 x 36 cm.
11 x 14 in.

Federal Writers Project Posters

Among the many groups adversely affected by the Depression-age economy were the nation's writers. The works created by the Federal Writers Project (FWP) still serve today as accurate, evocative chronicles of this chapter in American history.

Between 1935 and 1943, the FWP, employing writers such as Richard Wright, Studs Terkel, Kenneth Rexroth, Nelson Algren, Ralph Ellison, and Conrad Aiken, produced hundreds of volumes of state and local histories. The American Guide Series served several purposes. They were lively, highly readable guidebooks meant for the general public, which, because they were local histories, boosted citizen pride at a time when Americans sorely needed such infusions of spirit. Derived from research in state and municipal archives by the FWP's Historical Records Survey Division, they were also significant historical documents: in the course of the research, for example, many archival collections were catalogued for the first time; frequently the guidebooks represented the first modern history of a locality; and residents were interviewed, their oral histories becoming an integral part of the guidebooks. Often reprinted today, the FWP guidebooks remain fascinating chronicles of the facts, tall tales, events and personalities that shaped America.

The guidebooks were only one type of work created by the writers of the FWP. Their output was diverse and included radio plays, an anthology of project members' prose and verse called **American Stuff**, and a series of more than thirty elementary-school science texts with such titles as **Looking at the Moon**, **Life in an Ant Hill**, and **The Romance of Rubber**. These works were among the many finished manuscripts offered by the FWP to U.S. government agencies and commercial publishing houses for printing and distribution.

253
This display case exhibits only a small number of the volumes produced by the FWP.

■

254
Galic
Chicago, IL
56 x 36 cm.
22 x 14 in.

255
Sidney Jacobson
(attributed)
New York, NY
56 x 36 cm.
22 x 14 in.

WPA-produced posters were used to
promote the work of the Federal Writers
Project and often the illustrations were
adapted from the cover art of the books
they advertised.

256
Artist unknown
Pennsylvania
56 x 36 cm.
22 x 14 in.

257
Sidney Jacobson
New York, NY
36 x 28 cm.
14 x 11 in.

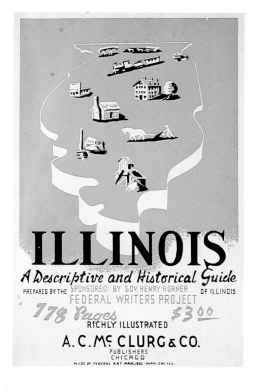

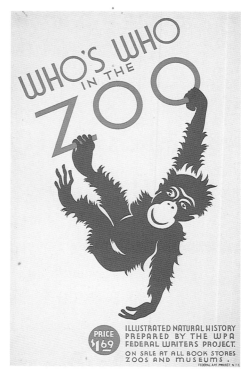

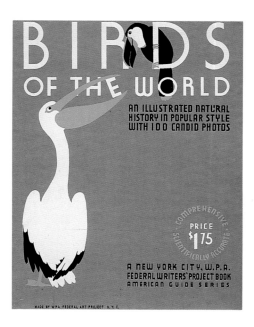

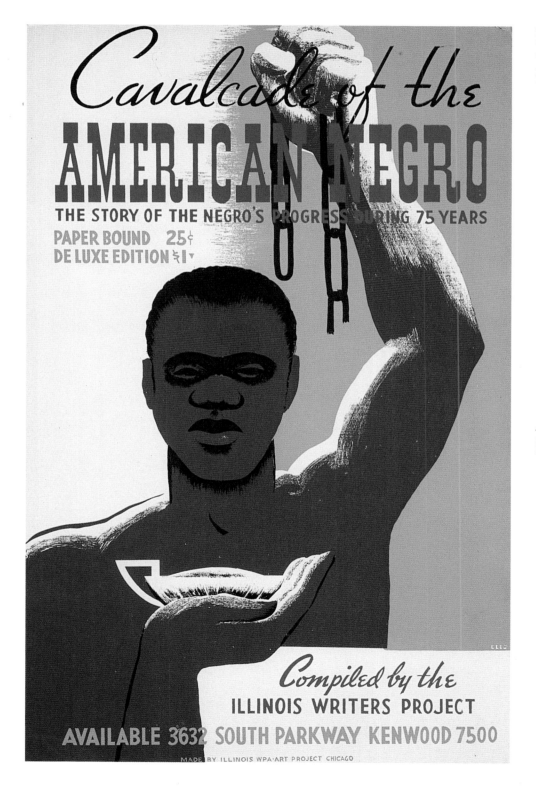

258
Cleo Sara
Chicago, IL
56 x 36 cm.
22 x 14 in.

A powerful image whose elements (up-raised fist, broken chain) prefigure "Black Power" posters of the late 1960s.

■

259
Homer Ansley
Northern California
61 x 51 cm.
24 x 20 in.

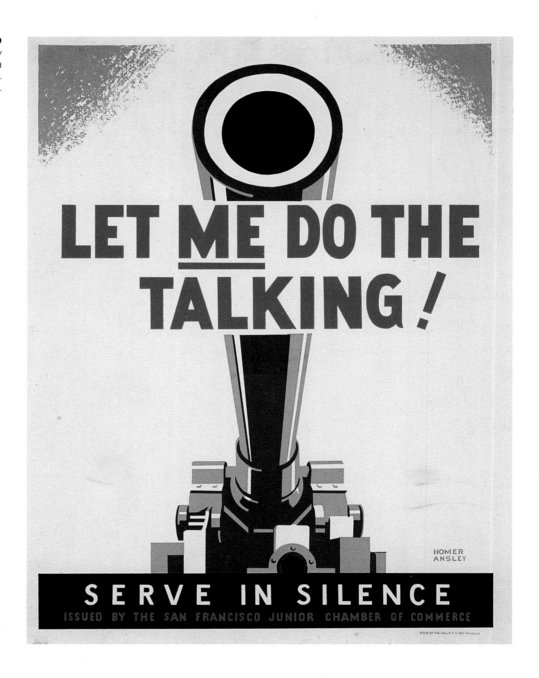

■

World War II Posters

In the early 1940s, as the United States entered World War II, increasingly stringent employment regulations and lack of funding forced the WPA projects to curtail their activities. Indeed, only the contributions of the FAP to the home-front war effort allowed it to stay alive. As a result, creative art was largely replaced by practical art.

Artists who had been experimenting in designs and techniques for producing visually powerful posters now turned their energies to creating charts for aircraft and uniform identification, menus for officers' mess halls, camp insignias, and window displays—works that were aesthetically weaker and more crudely executed than the prewar designs. They did produce some vivid and effective World War II propaganda art (although some of it bore racist depictions of Japanese). However, many of the works aiding the war effort were created by artists new to poster design. This dearth of training in the graphic arts often resulted in posters lacking the sophistication and subtlety of the poster divisions' earlier efforts.

Given the nation's ever-increasing channeling of its resources into the war effort, as well as continued opposition from the conservative congressional opponents to "make-work" and "boon-doggling," it was probably inevitable that the WPA/FAP would die. This it did, finally, in 1943. As President Roosevelt stated it, the WPA had served with distinction and "earned its honorable discharge."

260
This "Buy Bonds" booth was produced by silkscreen printmakers as one of their contributions to the homefront war effort.

261
Charles Pollock
Detroit, MI
77 x 64 cm.
30 x 25 in.

262
Edward T. Grigware
Washington
36 x 28 cm.
14 x 11 in.

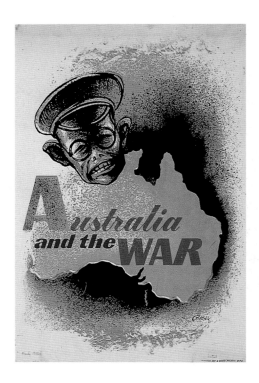

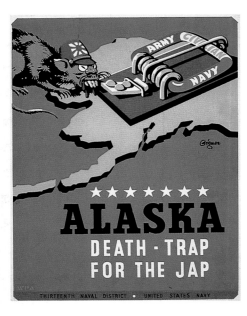

263
Russell W. Kraus
St. Louis, MO
61 x 51 cm.
24 x 20 in.

264
Phil von Phul
Washington
36 x 28 cm.
14 x 11 in.

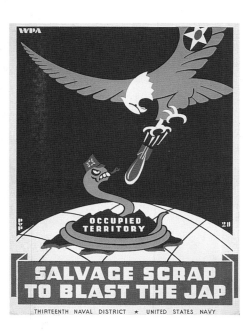

265
Russell W. Kraus
St. Louis, MO
61 x 51 cm.
24 x 20 in.

These posters [263, 264, 265] informed civilians about the contributions they could make to the war effort.

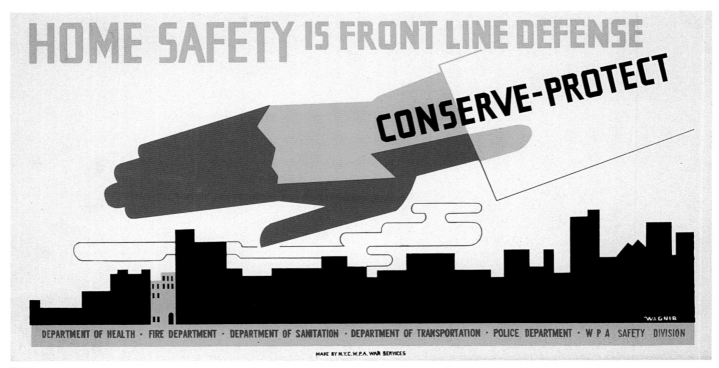

266
John Wagner
New York, NY
28 x 53 cm.
11 x 21 in.

267
B.E.N. (signed)
New York, NY
56 x 36 cm.
22 x 14 in.

268
Artist unknown
New York, NY
56 x 36 cm.
22 x 14 in.

269
Charlotte Angus
Philadelphia, PA
61 x 51 cm.
24 x 20 in.

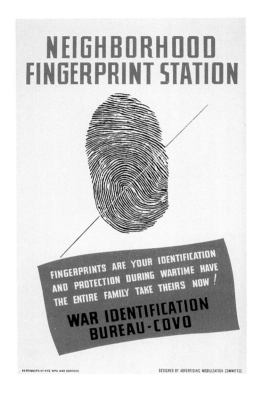

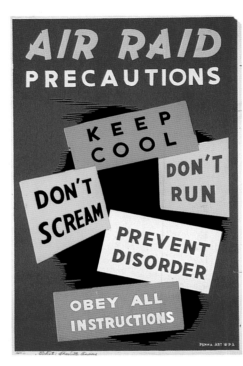

270
Welch
Alabama
71 x 56 cm.
28 x 22 in.

271
C.H. (signed)
Oakland, CA
61 x 46 cm.
24 x 18 in.

272
J.P. (signed)
New York, NY
56 x 36 cm.
22 x 14 in.

273
Louis Hirshman
Philadelphia, PA
61 x 46 cm.
24 x 18 in.

The rising sun motif and horrific image
of a Japanese soldier dominate this poster.
"Fag Bags" were for the safe disposal of
cigarettes and matches.

STOP
AND GET YOUR FREE FAG BAG

careless matches aid the Axis

274
William B. Finley
St. Louis, MO
51 x 61 cm.
20 x 24 in.

275
Vera Bock
New York, NY
71 x 56 cm.
28 x 22 in.

FEDERAL ART PROJECT

Portfolio Introduction

From among the many artists who created posters for the FAP / WAP nationwide, a small number have been selected for special recognition in this portfolio. Several factors have been considered in selecting the artists featured here, including that:

- Posters could be identified as the work of a particular artist.
- There was a sufficient number of identified posters available to allow a representative display of an artist's work.
- The work represents the qualities of good poster art by conveying a message through effective design and color.
- Information was available documenting that artist's career.

Identifying the designers responsible for the creation of individual posters was the first task to be undertaken, since many works are unsigned and entered institutional collections without attribution. Some identifications have been confirmed by referring to FAP exhibition catalogues. The author has made certain attributions, basing his judgement on stylistic similarities and other clues. Others have been made with the assistance of WPA poster artists, who reviewed their work and the work of their colleagues. Many posters, however, remain uncredited. The authors and publishers hope that, with this publication, additional identifications will be forthcoming.

Each of the featured artists has produced exemplary designs, which add substantially to the body of work that comprises the history of poster design in America. Many other artists, represented with extraordinary work in this book, are excluded from this portfolio only due to lack of biographical information. These include Albert Bender, Harry Herzog, Stanley Clough, and Jack Rivolta.

■

Vera Bock

276
Vera Bock cutting stencils for her poster
WPA Kills Rumors [275], circa 1938.

Born 1905, St. Petersburg, Russia.

At the onset of the Russian Revolution Vera Bock emigrated to the United States with her mother, a Russian-born concert pianist, and her father, an American banker. Her art education included trips to Europe, where she studied drawing and painting, and a year's stay in England during which she learned printing, photoengraving, manuscript illuminating, and wood engraving.

In 1929 she began to work as a book illustrator with two children's books, Ella Young's **The Tangle-Coated Horse** and Waldemer Bonsels' **The Adventures of Maya the Bee**. Throughout her career she illustrated children's books and many of these drawings are housed in the Kerlan Collection of Children's Literature at the University of Minnesota.

Vera Bock's silkscreened posters are notable for their distinctive woodblock-like appearance. Strong, solid forms, often Germanic in influence [frontispiece], dominate her designs. Her formation in book design and illustration is apparent in her series of posters, **History of Civic Services** [177-181]. In these designs, numerous human figures share space with well-executed typography, suggesting a quality of wonder often associated with children's books.

She was affiliated with the FAP from 1936 to 1939 as a member of the New York City poster division. During the 1940s she worked as an illustrator at **Life** and **Coronet** magazines. She continued to produce book illustration and design including **Little Magic Horse** (1942), **A Ring and A Riddle** (1944), and **A Critical History of Children's Literature** (1953).

Her work has been included in exhibitions at The New York Public Library (1942), The Art Directors Club (1946), "The International Exhibition of Illustrated Books" (The Pierpont Morgan Library, 1946), and "Ten Years of American Illustration" (The New York Public Library, 1951).

277
New York, NY
71 x 46 cm.
28 x 18 in.

278
New York, NY
71 x 46 cm.
28 x 18 in.

279
New York, NY
71 x 46 cm.
28 x 18 in.

280
New York, NY
71 x 56 cm.
28 x 22 in.

Richard Floethe

281
Richard Floethe, circa 1938.

Born 1901, Essen, Germany.

Floethe was educated in Germany where he studied at the Dortmund Art School, the Munich State School of Art, and the Bauhaus in Weimar.

His own poster designs strongly reflect his training at the Bauhaus, in such elements as the typeface Stencil, designed by Josef Albers, which he often used [283-285]. As administrator / art director of the New York City FAP poster division from 1936 to 1939, Floethe was viewed by designers as an encouraging, compassionate figure who provided a working environment in which artists were free to experiment and create.

Richard Floethe spent much of his career as a book illustrator. He has designed or illustrated over fifty books including **Ballet Shoes** (1937), **Picture Book of the Earth** (1949), and **Ting-a-Ling Tales** (1955). His designs and illustrations for **Tyl Ulenspiegl** (1935) and **Pinocchio** (1938) won the Limited Editions Club Prize. He has also illustrated books written by his wife, Louise Floethe. Among these titles are **If I Were Captain** (1956) and **Winning Colt** (1956).

Floethe's work was shown in "The 50 Books of the Year" exhibitions sponsored by the Society of Graphic Arts in 1934 and 1936. His work as a printmaker (woodcuts and serigraphs) is included in the collections of the Metropolitan Museum of Art, the Philadelphia Museum of Art, and the Kerlan Collection of the University of Minnesota.

Floethe taught commercial design at the Cooper Union School of Art (1941–1942) and illustration at the Ringling School of Art (1955–1967).

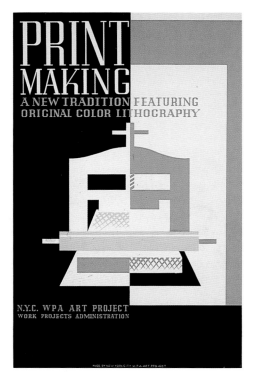

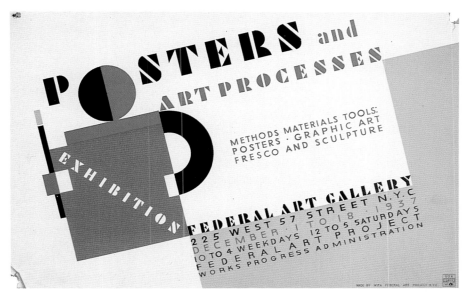

282
New York, NY
56 x 36 cm.
22 x 14 in.

283
New York, NY
36 x 56 cm.
14 x 22 in.

284
New York, NY
56 x 36 cm.
22 x 14 in.

285
New York, NY
56 x 36 cm.
22 x 14 in.

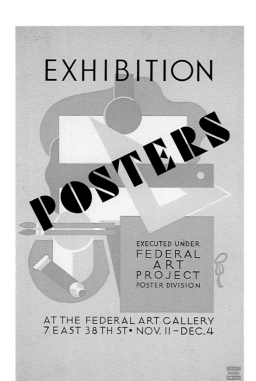

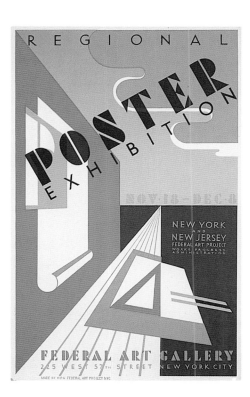

Richard Halls

286
Richard Halls, circa 1940.

Born 1906, New Orleans, Louisiana; died 1976, Huntington Station, New York.

Richard Halls' early years were spent traveling through the U.S. and Europe with his father, a sculptor whose commissions included many public monuments. After training at the Cleveland Institute of Art (graduated with honors, 1928), Halls worked with painter and designer Charles Burchfield, 1928–1929.

Halls joined the FAP from 1936 to 1939 where he created many posters for the Federal Theatre Project. His designs often contain playful, comic features.

After World War II service and studies at the Art Center College of Design, Halls began to work as a freelance illustrator, but a part-time job as instructor at City College of New York redirected him to a career in education. From 1952 to 1976 Halls taught advertising art and design on the faculty of the State University of New York at Farmingdale. He received his B.A. from Adelphi University in 1961.

Halls' paintings, watercolors, and pochoir (stencil) prints were included in exhibitions at the Cleveland Museum of Art (1934), the Brooklyn Museum (1936), and the American Watercolor Society (1952).

287
New York, NY
56 x 36 cm.
22 x 14 in.

288
New York, NY
56 x 36 cm.
22 x 14 in.

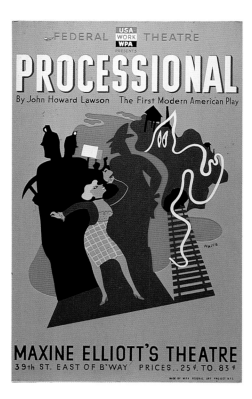

289
New York, NY
56 x 36 cm.
22 x 14 in.

290
New York, NY
56 x 36 cm.
22 x 14 in.

Robert M. Jones

291
Bob Jones, circa 1938.

Born 1913, Goff, Kansas.

Bob Jones created posters for a WPA project far from the mainstream of the commercial art world. He was employed by the State Art Center in Salt Lake City during 1939 and 1940 as poster maker, exhibit designer, and photographer. Jones not only designed materials to advertise the center but as photographer documented its activities. His photographs and spot illustrations are also included in the Federal Writers Project, **Utah, A Guide to the State**, published in 1941.

Jones was educated at the University of Utah and the California School of Fine Art before joining the WPA.

After leaving the Utah FAP in 1940, Jones established his career in New York City where he worked for **Life** magazine and Columbia Records. He was art director for RCA Records from 1953 to 1973.

Jones' work was included in exhibitions sponsored by the American Institute of Graphic Arts, the New York Art Directors Club, and the Society of Typographic Arts. Over twenty one-person exhibitions of his work have been held in the course of his career.

Bob Jones' art has received more than 200 awards from organizations such as the Society of Illustrators, the Type Directors Club, the American Institute of Graphic Arts, **Graphis**, and **Communication Arts** magazines. In addition, Jones has won nineteen nominations and six Grammys for best album cover from the National Academy of Recording Arts and Sciences.

Jones was an instructor at the Cooper Union School of Art 1951– 1953 and the University of Connecticut 1972–1974. He currently operates a letterpress printing studio, Glad Hand Press, in Stamford, Connecticut.

■

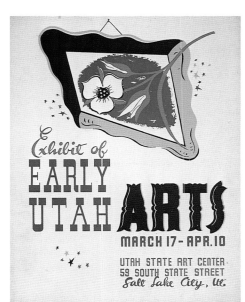

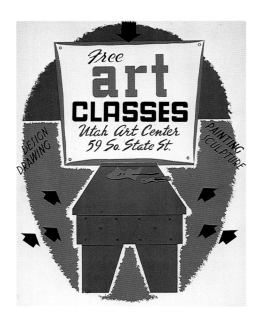

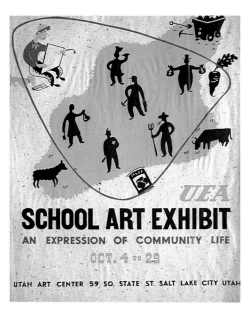

292
Salt Lake City, UT
36 x 28 cm.
14 x 11 in.

293
Salt Lake City, UT
36 x 28 cm.
14 x 11 in.

294
Salt Lake City, UT
36 x 28 cm.
14 x 11 in.

295
Salt Lake City, UT
36 x 28 cm.
14 x 11 in.

Erik Hans Krause

296
Erik Hans Krause, circa 1938.

Born 1899, Halle-Salle, Germany.

Erik Hans Krause began his career in Germany after graduating from the Academy of Decorative Arts and Crafts in Dresden. Following his move to the United States in 1923, Krause worked in advertising in New York City. He moved permanently to Rochester, New York in 1932 and beginning in 1936 was employed with the FAP there, supervising ten artists and craftsmen and designing textiles and posters.

Since his years with the WPA, Krause has attained national prominence as a painter of botanical subjects. Exhibitions of his work have been held at the Smithsonian Institution, the National Audubon Society, the United States National Arboretum, and the Rochester Museum and Science Center.

His work has been honored by the American Institute of Graphic Arts and by the University of Rochester with its Fairchild Award in 1938. Krause's illustrations have appeared in **National Audubon** and **National Horticultural** magazines. Krause has taught design and illustration at the Rochester Institute of Technology.

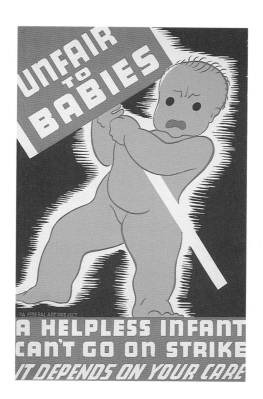

297
Rochester, NY
56 x 36 cm.
22 x 14 in.

298
Rochester, NY
56 x 36 cm.
22 x 14 in.

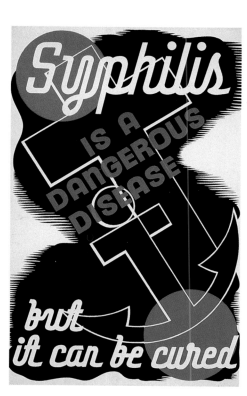

299
Rochester, NY
56 x 36 cm.
22 x 14 in.

300
Rochester, NY
56 x 36 cm.
22 x 14 in.

Katherine Milhous

301
Katherine Milhous, circa 1945.

Born 1894, Philadelphia, Pennsylvania; died 1977, Philadelphia, Pennsylvania.

Katherine Milhous created some of the most distinctive posters produced by the WPA. She was a supervisor of the FAP in Philadelphia (her birthplace and lifelong home) from 1935 to 1940. Milhous often incorporated the folk traditions of the Pennsylvania Dutch communities in her poster designs. Her deep affection for the locality's history and people is apparent in her depictions of the Amish and Mennonites.

Milhous was educated at the Philadelphia Museum School of Industrial Art and the Pennsylvania Academy of the Fine Arts before joining the FAP. An exhibition of her posters in a FAP gallery attracted the attention of a children's book editor at Charles Scribner's Sons, where she was a staff designer 1944– 1946, and launched her successful career as an award-winning children's book illustrator.

In 1938 her first book as writer and illustrator, **Once Upon a Time**, was published. It was followed by other titles including **Snow Over Bethlehem** (1945), **With Bells On** (1955), and **Through These Arches: The Story of Independence Hall** (1964). She received the American Library Association's Caldecott Medal, honoring the most distinguished picture book for children, for **The Egg Tree** (1950).

Milhous was a member of the American Institute of Graphic Arts. Her work was exhibited at the 1939 New York World's Fair and at the Pennsylvania Academy of the Fine Arts.

302
Philadelphia, PA
53 x 42 cm.
21 x 16½ in.
Lithograph

303
Philadelphia, PA
64 x 48 cm.
25 x 19 in.
Woodblock

304
Philadelphia, PA
64 x 48 cm.
25 x 19 in.
Woodblock

305
Philadelphia, PA
54 x 43 cm.
21 x 17 in.
Lithograph

Jerome Henry Roth

306
Jerome Roth, circa 1935.

Born 1918, New York, New York.

Jerome Henry Roth (born Rothstein) joined the N.Y.C. poster division after graduating from high school in the Bronx and, at age 16, was the youngest member of the project. While working days for the WPA, Roth attended Art Students' League at night. He also studied at the New School for Social Research and graduated from the Pratt Institute.

Roth was employed by the FAP poster project from 1935 to 1939, when he left to join a New York City advertising agency. After serving in Europe during World War II as a B-15 navigator, he returned to New York in the late 1940s and worked as a graphics assistant to designer Herbert Bayer. In the early 1950s Roth formed his own design studio, which he operated until his retirement in 1983. He has taught at the Fashion Institute of Technology and the College of the City of New York.

He continues to paint and has had a number of exhibitions at Kaufmann Gallery, N.Y.C.; the Garrison Art Center, Garrison; the Silvermine Guild of Galleries, Canaan, Ct.; and the Overseas Press Club, N.Y.C.

307
New York, NY
56 x 36 cm.
22 x 14 in.

308
New York, NY
56 x 36 cm.
22 x 14 in.

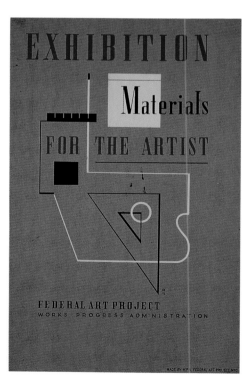

309
New York, NY
71 x 56 cm.
28 x 22 in.

310
New York, NY
56 x 36 cm.
22 x 14 in.

Anthony Velonis

311
Anthony Velonis, circa 1939.

Born 1911, New York, New York.

Anthony Velonis introduced the silkscreen process to the WPA poster division in New York City. His pamphlet, **Technical Problems of the Artist: Technique of the Silk Screen Process**, published in 1937, allowed other poster projects around the country to utilize this technique.

Velonis graduated from New York University's School of Fine Arts and joined Mayor LaGuardia's poster project in New York City in 1934. In 1935 this project came under federal sponsorship and Velonis remained with the division until 1938. After leaving the poster division, Velonis worked in the FAP graphic art division where he continued to experiment with silk-screening techniques and taught fellow artists about the process.

Velonis' poster designs are marked by cubist-influenced elements and his experiments with printing techniques: split-font applications of paint [312], and applications of tusche crayon directly to the screen.

In 1939 Velonis and Hyman Warsager founded the Creative Printmakers Group and in the late 1940s he started the Ceraglass Company, an industrial silkscreening firm, which pioneered methods of silkscreen printing on glass and plastic containers.

Velonis' art has been exhibited at the Weyhe Gallery, New York City (1940), the Springfield Museum of Fine Arts (1940), the Philadelphia Museum of Art (1971), and the Brooklyn Museum (1986). His prints are included in the collections of the National Museum of American Art, the Metropolitan Museum of Art, the Australian National Gallery and others.

Anthony Velonis currently lives in New Jersey and continues to work as a printmaker and painter.

■

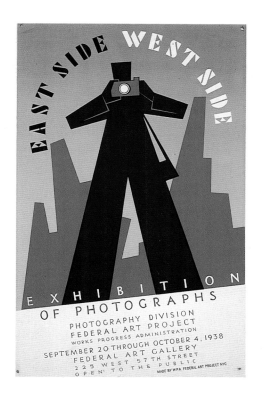

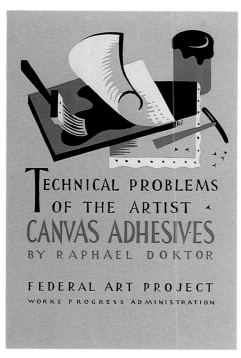

312
New York, NY
56 x 36 cm.
22 x 14 in.

313
Pamphlet cover
New York, NY
22 x 14.5 cm.
8¾ x 5¾ in.

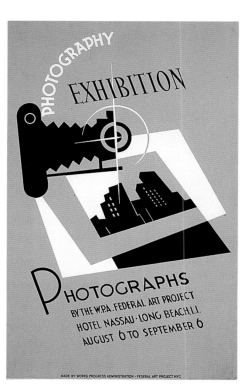

314
New York, NY
71 x 56 cm.
28 x 22 in.

315
New York, NY
56 x 36 cm.
22 x 14 in.

Harry Herzog

Ben Kaplan

Richard Halls

Richard Halls

Aida McKenzie

Alex Dux

This calendar marks a transitional stage in the development of the silkscreen as a graphic arts method. The illustrations and printing techniques show the artists' growing command of the medium. Technically, these prints move away from the generally flat, blocky areas of color used in early designs toward a looser, painterly application of color found in later serigraphs. It was produced for distribution to members of Congress and the administration. Richard Floethe discusses the controversy that it created in his remembrance, page 130.

■

JULY

Richard Halls

AUGUST

Vera Bock

SEPTEMBER

Richard Halls

OCTOBER

Bryan Burroughs

NOVEMBER

Ben Kaplan

DECEMBER

Jerome Roth (Rothstein)

316
1939 WPA / FAP Calendar
Art direction and design by Richard Floethe
Front cover design [26] by Jerome Roth
New York, NY
28 x 22 cm.
11 x 8⁵/₈ in.

Selected Bibliography

WPA / FEDERAL ART PROJECT

Bermingham, Peter. **The New Deal in the Southwest: Arizona and New Mexico.** Tucson: University of Arizona Museum of Art, 1977.

Bloxom, Marguerite D. **Pickaxe and Pencil: References for the Study of the WPA.** Washington, D.C.: Library of Congress, 1982.

Brown, Lorraine, and John O'Connor. **Free, Adult, Uncensored: The Living History of the Federal Theatre Project.** Washington, D.C.: New Republic Books, 1978.

Bruce, Edward, and Forbes Watson. **Mural Designs, 1934–1936. Art in Federal Buildings, volume 1.** Washington, D.C.: Art in Federal Buildings Incorporated, 1936.

Craven, Thomas. **A Treasury of American Prints.** New York: Simon and Schuster, 1939.

Flanagan, Hallie. **Arena.** New York: Duell, Sloan and Pearce, 1940.

Jewett, Masha Zakheim. **Coit Tower San Francisco: Its History and Art.** San Francisco: Volcano Press. 1983.

McDonald, William F. **Federal Relief Administration and the Arts.** Columbus: Ohio State University Press, 1969.

McKinzie, Richard D. **The New Deal for Artists.** Princeton, New Jersey: Princeton University Press, 1973.

Mangione, Jerre. **The Dream and the Deal: The Federal Writers Project, 1935–1943.** Boston: Little Brown and Company, 1972.

Marling, Karal Ann. **Wall-to-Wall America: A Cultural History of Post-Office Murals in the Great Depression.** Minneapolis: University of Minnesota Press, 1982.

Markowitz, Gerald E., and Marlene Park. **New Deal for Art: the Government Art Projects of the 1930s with Examples from New York City and State.** New York: Gallery Association of New York State, Inc., 1977.

———. **Post Offices and Public Art in the New Deal.** Philadelphia: Temple University Press, 1985.

Meltzer, Milton. **Violins and Shovels: The WPA Arts Projects.** New York: Delacorte Press, 1976.

New Horizons in American Art. New York: Museum of Modern Art, 1936.

O'Connor, Francis V., ed. **Art for the Millions: Essays from the 1930s by Artists and Administrators of the WPA Federal Art Project.** Boston: New York Graphic Society, 1975.

———. **Federal Art Patronage: 1933–1943.** College Park, Maryland: University of Maryland Art Gallery, 1966.

———. **Federal Support for the Visual Arts: The New Deal and Now.** Greenwich, Connecticut: New York Graphic Society, 1969.

WPA / FAP Graphics. Washington, D.C.: Smithsonian Institution Press, 1976.

NEW DEAL ERA

American Artists' Congress. **Graphic Works of the American Thirties.** Reprint of **America Today: A Book of 100 Prints**, 1936. New York: Da Capo Press, 1977.

Anderson, Edward. **Hungry Men.** New York: Penguin, 1985.

Appel, Benjamin. **The People Talk.** New York: E.P. Dutton and Company, Inc., 1940.

Baigell, Matthew. **The American Scene: American Paintings of the 1930s.** New York: Praeger Publications, 1974.

———, and Julia Williams. **Artists Against War and Fascism: Papers of the First American Artist's Congress.** New Brunswick, New Jersey: Rutgers University Press, 1986.

Banks, Ann. **First Person America.** New York: Alfred A. Knopf, Inc., 1980.

Bourke-White, Margaret, and Erskine Caldwell. **You Have Seen Their Faces.** New York: Viking Press, 1937. Reprint. New York: Arno Press, 1975.

Federal Writers Project. **These are Our Lives.** Chapel Hill, North Carolina: University of North Carolina Press, 1939.

Halper, Albert. **Union Square.** New York: Viking Press, 1933.

McElvaine, Robert S. **Down and Out in the Great Depression: Letters from the Forgotten Man.** Chapel Hill, North Carolina: University of North Carolina Press, 1983.

MacLeish, Archibald, **Land of the Free.** Reprint, with introduction by A.D. Coleman. New York: Da Capo Press, 1977.

O'Neal, Hank. **A Vision Shared: A Classic Portrait of America and its People. 1935–1943.** New York: St. Martin's Press, 1976.

Stryker, Roy E., and Nancy Wood. **In This Proud Land: America 1935–1943 Seen in the FSA Photographs.** Boston: New York Graphic Society, 1973.

Terkel, Studs. **Hard Times: An Oral History of the Great Depression.** New York: Pantheon, 1970.

POSTERS

Ades, Dawn. **The 20th-Century Poster: Design of the Avant-Garde.** New York: Abbeville Press, 1984.

Barnicott, John. **A Concise History of Posters.** New York: Harry N. Abrams, Inc., 1972.

Constantine, Mildred, and Alan M. Fern. **Word and Image: Posters from the Collection of the Museum of Modern Art.** New York: Museum of Modern Art, 1968.

Friedman, Jeannie. "WPA Poster Project: When Government Sponsors Art." **Print**, July / August 1978.

Gallo, Max. **The Poster in History.** New York: American Heritage Publishing Co., Inc., 1974.

Hillier, Bevis. **Posters.** New York: Stein and Day, 1969.

Reproduction Credits

Hutchison, Harold F. **The Poster: An Illustrated History from 1860.** New York: The Viking Press, 1968.

Kellner, Sidney. "Federal Art Project Posters Develop New Art Forms." **Signs of the Times,** April 1938.

Margolin, Victor, Ira Brichta, and Vivian Brichta. **The Promise and the Product: 200 Years of American Advertising Posters.** New York: Macmillan Publishing Co., Inc., 1979.

Rhodes, Anthony. **Propaganda, the Art of Persuasion: World War II.** New York: Chelsea House Publishers, 1976.

Rickards, Maurice. **The Rise and Fall of the Poster.** New York: McGraw-Hill Book Company, 1971.

Rossi, Attilio. **Posters.** New York: Paul Hamlyn Publishing Group Limited, 1969.

Sacartoff, Elizabeth. "WPA's First-Class Posters Make First-Class Salesmen." **P.M. Weekly,** August 17, 1941.

Weill, Alain. **The Poster: A Worldwide Survey and History.** Boston: G.K. Hall and Co., 1985.

SILKSCREEN PROCESS
Biegeleisen, J.I., and E.J. Busenbark. **The Silk Screen Printing Process.** New York: McGraw-Hill Book Company, Inc., 1938.

Biegeleisen, J.I., and Max Arthur Cohn. **Silk Screen Stenciling as a Fine Art.** New York: McGraw-Hill Book Company, Inc., 1942.

Shokler, Harry. **Artist's Manual for Silk Screen Print Making.** New York: American Artists Group, 1946.

Sternberg, Harry. **Silk Screen Color Printing.** New York: McGraw-Hill Book Company, Inc., 1942.

Velonis, Anthony. "Silk Screen Process Prints." **Magazine of Art,** July 1940.

————. Technical Problems of the Artist: Technique of the Silk Screen Process. New York: New York City WPA Art Project, n.d.

Williams, Reba, and David Williams. "The Early History of the Screenprint." **Print Quarterly,** December, 1986.

Zigrosser, Carl. "The Serigraph, a New Medium." **Print Collectors Quarterly,** December 1941.

————. "Ten Years of Serigraphy." **The New Colophon,** January, 1948.

Numbers listed below refer to figure numbers. All figures are used with permission.

Author's Collection
5, 9, 10, 13, 16–19, 24, 28, 46, 130, 132, 134, 237, 259, 266, 287

Richard Floethe
20, 281

Eunice Halls
286

Pavelle Jacobs / Fortune Magazine / Time, Inc.
88

Bob Jones
291–295

Kerlan Collection, University of Minnesota
301

Erik Hans Krause
296

Library of Congress, Federal Theatre Collection, George Mason University, Fairfax, Virginia
90, 91, 93, 96–101, 103–105, 108, 110, 112, 114, 116, 119–125, 197, 289, 290

Library of Congress, Prints and Photographs Division
Front cover, frontispiece, 1–4, 6, 8, 30–32, 34–45, 47–78, 87, 89, 92, 94, 95, 102, 106, 107, 109, 111, 115, 117, 118, 131, 133, 135–196, 198–236, 239–252, 254–258, 261–265, 267–275, 277–280, 282–285, 288, 297–300, 302–305, 307, 309, 312, 314, 315, back cover

Municipal Archives, Department of Records and Information Services, City of New York
253

National Archives
7, 14, 15, 22, 25, 26, 33, 238, 260, 276

Native American Painting Reference Library. Private Collection
80, 82–84

New York Daily News
23

Jerome H. Roth
306, 308, 310

Louis B. Siegriest
86

Elizabeth Timberman / Life Magazine ©1944 Time, Inc.
29

Anthony Velonis
12, 21, 126–129, 311, 313

Vizcarra Collection
79, 81, 85, 113

The Mitchell Wolfson Jr. Collection of Decorative and Propaganda Arts, Miami-Dade Community College
27, 316

All reasonable efforts to find and secure repro-duction rights have been made by the author. Any omissions or errors are inadvertent and the publisher will be pleased to make any corrections in future printings if notified.

Posters referenced by state. Numbers listed below refer to figure numbers.

Alabama
270

California
79–86, 99–100, 109, 259, 271

Connecticut
113–114

Illinois
2, 4, 39–40, 48, 52, 53, 55, 59, 61, 63, 66–68, 74, 76, 119, 145–146, 151–157, 159–164, 166–169, 172–176, 183, 186, 196, 199, 203–205, 230, 244, 246, 254, 258

Iowa
56, 70–72, 182, 192, 198, 247

Massachusetts
3, 30, 34–37, 41, 57–58, 62, 64, 73, 104, 112, 125

Michigan
120, 189, 261

Missouri
111, 263, 265, 274

New Jersey
69

New York
frontispiece, 1, 6, 8, 42–44, 47, 49–50, 65, 75, 77–78, 87, 89, 90–92, 94–98, 101, 103–105, 107–108, 110, 115–117, 130–137, 141–144, 148, 158, 170–171, 177–181, 184–185, 187–188, 191, 193–195, 202, 206–209, 215–223, 227–228, 234, 239–243, 245, 248–252, 255, 257, 266–268, 272, 275, 277–280, 282–285, 287–290, 297–300, 307–310, 312–315

Ohio
35, 51, 54, 60, 102, 147, 149–150, 190, 200–201, 224–226, 229, 232

Pennsylvania
31, 45, 93, 138–140, 165, 210, 213, 231, 233, 235–236, 256, 269, 273, 302–305

Utah
32, 292–295

Washington
106, 262, 264

Index

Bold page numbers indicate illustrations.

Abstract art, 24, 111
Agha, Dr. Mehemed Fehmy, 109
Aiken, Conrad, 138
Albers, Josef, 21
Algren, Nelson, 139
American Guide Series, 139
Angus, Charlotte
  poster by, **148**
Anish, Blanche L.
  poster by, **106**
Ansley, Homer
  poster by, **142**
Armory Show of 1913, 108
Art Directors Club of New York, 108
Artists' Union, 72, 73
Bacon, Ernst, 133
Barnet, Will, 15, 30, 46
Bauhaus, 9, 24, 25, 37, 108, 109,
  129, 130, 134
Bayer, Herbert, 109
Beard
  posters by, **89, 95**
Bechter, Fred, 128
Bender, Albert M., 153
  poster attributed to, **111**
  posters by, **88, 90, 91, 93**
Benito, Edouardo, 110
Benn, Ben, 31
Binder, Joseph, 24, 110
  design production, photo of, **30**
Blacks
  in Federal Theatre Project, 57, 67
  posters of, **64, 67, 135, 141**
Block, Paul, 73
Bock, Vera, 129
  biography, 154
  FAP calendar design, **171**
  poster attributed to, **48**
  posters by, **2, 67, 100–101,
  125, 152, 155**
Borowski, Felix, 133
Bowles, Paul, 133
Breitenbach, Edgar, 33, 35
Brodovich, Alexy, 109
Brooks, James, 10
Browder, Earl, 72
Brown, Samuel
  poster by, **88**
Browne, Byron, 75
Buczak, John
  posters by, **51, 94, 99**
Burroughs, Bryan, 129
  FAP calendar design, **171**
  posters by, **132, 133**
Calder, Alexander, 21
Capek, Karel, 65
Carborundum prints, 37

Carken
  posters by, **97, 135**
Cassandre, A.M., 24, 74, 110
Castellano, Federico, 78
Chaney, Ruth, 21, 76
  photo with serigraph, **27**
Chicago Historical Society
  poster collection, 32
Chicago Poster Division, 17, 19, 22
Children's art education, 44
  posters for **92**
Civic activity posters, **86–107**
Civilian Works Administration
  (CWA), 14, 17, 18, 73
Cleveland Public Library
  poster collection, 33
Clough, Stanley T., 153
  posters by, **39, 43, 46, 89, 121**
Coiner, Charles T.
  photo of, with NRA symbol, **17**
Community Art Centers (WPA),
  16, 44
Constructivism, 24, 110, 134
Cotten, Joseph, 57
Creative Printmakers Group, 73,
  77–78
Cubism, 9, 108, 110
Dassin, Jules, 57
Davis, Stuart, 9, 15, 21, 30, 74
DeColas, Emanuel
  poster by, **58**
de Coursey, Nell, 128
de Kooning, Willem, 15, 43
Defense Department
  FAP transferred to, 31
Dehn, Adolph, 78
Delaney, Robert Miles, 133
Depression, 13, 28, 72
Design Laboratory, 37
De Stijl, 9
DeYoung Museum (San Francisco)
  poster exhibition (1939), **37**
Dies, Martin, 26–27
Dies committee, 26–27
Diller, Burgoyne, 130
Dusek, Joseph
  poster by, **7**
Dux, Alexander
  FAP calendar design, **170**
  poster by, **83**
Dwight, Mabel, 46
Easel paintings, 43
Education posters, **86–107**
Eichenberg, Fritz, 46
Ellison, Ralph, 139
Engel, A. Lehman, 133
Evergood, Philip, 74

Federal Art Project (FAP), 7–10,
  14–35, 73, 77, 79, 128–130
  calendar, 32, 130, **170–171**
  decline of, 26–32, 143
  graphic art division, 20, 76, 130
  logo variations, 40–41
  poster division, 17–26, 73, 128
Federal Dance Project (FDP), 133
  posters for, **137**
Federal Music Project (FMP)
  posters for, 14, **133–137**
Federal Project Number One, 14
Federal Theatre Project (FTP), 14,
  22, 27, 28–29, 32, 57
  Negro Theatre Unit, 59, 67
  posters at George Mason
  University, 32
  posters for, 22, 23, **56–71**
Federal Writers Project (FWP), 14,
  22, 26
  book jackets for, 22
  posters for, **138–141**
Fern, Alan, 8
Finley, William B.
  poster by, **151**
Flanagan, Hallie, 57
Floethe, Richard, 9, 25, 73–74,
  79, 171
  biography, 156
  photos of, **25, 156**
  posters by, **42, 43, 131, 157**
  self-portrait, **128**
Fogel, Seymour, 10
Galic
  posters by, **99, 140**
Gebrauchsgraphik, 109
George Mason University
  FAP posters at, 32
Glickman, Maurice
  poster of sculpture by, **48**
Godsoe, Robert, 130
Golden Gate International
  Exposition (1939)
  posters for, **54–55**
Gottlieb, Harry, 21, 46, 76
  serigraph, **33**
Graham, Ralph, 19, 134
Greeting card design, **22**
Gregg, Arlington
  posters by, **46, 93, 96**
Grigware, Edward
  poster by, **144**
Gropius, Walter, 25, 109
Guston, Philip, 10
Halls, Richard, 75, 129, 131
  biography, 158
  FAP calendar designs, **170, 171**
  photo of, **158**
  poster attributed to, **63**
  posters by, **67, 83, 137, 159**

Harari, Hananiah, 74
Harnoncourt, René, 55
Hart, Frederic, 133
Health posters, 112–115,
  118–119, 122–123
Held, John, Jr., 110
Herzog, Harry, 129, 153
  FAP calendar design, **170**
  posters by, **58, 66, 84, 86,
  88, 106**
Hirshman, Louis
  poster by, **150**
House Investigation Committee, 26
Houseman, John, 56
Humfreville, Foster
  posters by, **15, 118**
Humphrey, Doris, 133
Huston, John, 57
Hyperion Press, 78
Index of American Design,
  47, 78, 130
Indian art posters, **52–55**
Jacobson, Sidney
  poster attributed to, **140**
  poster by, **140**
Jameson, Mitchell, 7
Jones, Robert M.
  biography, 160
  photo of, **160**
  posters by, **161**
Kallenberg, Alex
  posters by, **15, 115, 118**
Kandinsky, Wassily, 9, 25
Kaplan, Ben, 129
  FAP calendar designs, **170, 171**
  poster by, **122**
Katz, Morris
  poster by, **88**
Kaufman, Mortimer, 128
Kellner, Sidney, 23
Kessler, Herman
  poster attributed to, **120**
  poster by, **120**
Klee, Paul, 25, 78
Knotts, Ben, 78
Krasner, Lee, 14, 31, 43
Kraus, Russell W.
  posters by, **144, 145**
Krause, Erik Hans
  biography, 162
  photo of, **162**
  posters by, **163**
Kreger,
  posters by, **103**
Lachenmann, Robert
  poster by, **125**
La Guardia, Fiorello, 17, 31, 73

Lancaster, Burt, 57
Laning, Edward, 16
Lassen, Ben
	posters by, **68, 134**
Lawrence, Jacob, 43
LeBoit, Joseph, 76
Levine, Estelle
	posters by, **103, 121**
Lewitsky, Bella, 133
Library of Congress, 7, 8, 32, 33
Limón, José, 133
Living Newspaper, 57, 59
	posters, **58–59**
Long, Frank Weathers
	poster by, **96**
Losey, Joseph, 57
Lozowick, Louis, 21, 46, 76
Lumet, Sidney, 57
Maril, Herman, 7
Matthews, John
	poster by, **117**
McKenzie, Aida, 129
	FAP calendar design, **170**
	posters by, **61, 80**
McKnight-Kauffer, E., 24
McMahon, Audrey, 29, 73, 76,
	128, 130
Merlin
	poster by, **106**
Milhous, Katherine
	biography, 164
	photo of, **164**
	posters by, **36, 165**
Miller, Arthur, 57
Moholy-Nagy, Laszlo, 109
Morley, Eugene, 21, 74, 76
Mostel, Zero, 72
Motherwell, Robert, 21
Muchley, Robert
	posters by, **84, 116, 117**
Muller
	poster by, **120**
Murals, 7–10, 15
Nase, Allan
	poster by, **126**
Nason, Ben
	poster by, **46**
	posters attributed to, **38**
National Art Week (1940), 30
National Gallery of Art, 47
	WPA art exhibitions, 35
National Park Service
	wildlife posters, **97**
National Recovery Act
	symbol, **17**
National Youth Association, 87
Neel, Alice, 15, 43

Nevelson, Louise, 15
New York City Poster Division, 17,
	18–19, 22—25, 31, 73
	calendar by, **32**, 130, **170–171**
	photo, **15**
New York Historical Society
	poster collection, 33
Nicholson, Frank S.
	posters by, **83, 97, 108**
Nierendorff Gallery, 78
Olds, Elizabeth, 21, 46, 76
	poster by, **23**
Osborn, Erel
	posters by, **44, 47, 49, 51, 92**
Paintings, 43
Peck, Augustus, 76
Perkins, Frances, 79
Pettee, Walter C.
	poster by, **120**
Pistchal
	posters attributed to, **52, 53**
Plakate, Das, 109
Plattner, Max
	poster by, **115**
Pollock, Charles
	poster by, **144**
Pollock, Jackson, 15, 31, 43, 74
Posoff, Isadore
	poster by, **84**
Pratt, Herbert
	poster by, **60**
Printmaking processes, 37
Public housing posters, **120–121**
Public Use of Arts Committee,
	75–76
Public Works of Art Project, 14
Pytlak, Leonard, 76
Quinn, Thomas
	photo of, **73**
Rauschenberg, Robert, 21
Ray, Nicholas, 57
Rebay (von Ehrenweisen), Hilla, 74
Reed, John, 72
Refregier, Anton, 10
Reinhardt, Ad, 43, 74
Reminick, Harry
	poster by, **62**
Rexroth, Kenneth, 139
Rivera, Diego, 16
Rivolta, Jack, 153
	posters by, **14, 85, 109**
Roberts, Henry
	photo with FAP paintings, **34**
Rollins, Lloyd, 130
Roosevelt, Franklin Delano, 2, 13,
	14, 32, 79, 113

Roth (Rothstein), Jerome Henry,
	24, 129
	biography, 166
	calendar by, **32**
	FAP calendar design, **171**
	photo of, **166**
	posters by, **40, 82, 167**
Safety posters, **116–117, 124–127**
Sara, Cleo
	posters by, **93, 141**
Schafrank, Louis, 129
Schardt, Bernard, 21
Schnellock, Ned B.
	poster by, **92**
Schuler, Earl
	poster by, **125**
Serigraphy, 21, 37, 73, 77–78
Shahn, Ben, 10
Shaw, George Bernard, 68
Sheer, Ben
	poster by, **138**
Shepard, Otis, 24, 112
Sherman, Nathan
	posters by, **125, 127**
Shokler, Harry, 76–77
Short, Dewey, 26
Siegriest, Louis, B., 55
	posters by, **54–55**
Silkscreening, 18–22, 73, 75,
	109–110, 170
	exhibition, 24
	process illustrated, **20–21**
	school, 23
Social Realism, 28
Sokoloff, Nikolai, 133
Somervell, Colonel Brehon, 29, 30,
	78–79
Soyer, Raphael, 30
Spellens, Irving
	poster by, **58**
Steffens, Bernard, 76
Stella, Frank, 21
Sternberg, Harry, 30, 76
Stevenson, Hugh
	poster by, **96**
Stone lithography, 37
Surrealism, 108, 110
Synthetic cubism, 9
Tamiris, Helen, 133
Tartaglia, Angelo
	poster by, **49**
Tchachasov, Nahum, 74
Temporary Emergency Relief
	Administration (TERA), 14
Terkel, Studs, 138
Thomas, J. Parnell, 26
Thomas, Norman, 72

Thomson, Virgil, 57
Treasury Relief Art Project
	(TRAP), 15
U.S. Travel Bureau posters, **80–85**
Unemployed
	artists' demonstration,
		photo of, **16**
	march to Washington,
		photo of, **12**
Unemployment, 13
Vander Sluis, George
	poster by, **44**
Velonis, Anthony, 18, 29, 30,
	72, 129, 131
	biography, 168
	photos of, **73, 168**
	poster design, **25**
	posters by, **51, 64, 75, 169**
	print drying rack, photo of, **79**
	silkscreening pamphlet by, 19–22
Velonis, Constantine
	photo, **73**
Verschuuren, Charles
	posters by, **60, 103,
	114–115, 118**
von Groschwitz, Gustav, 130
von Phul, Phil
	poster by, **144**
Wagner, John
	posters by, **97, 120, 146**
Ward, Lynd, 76, 130
Warhol, Andy, 21
Warsager, Hyman, 21, 30, 76
	photo, **73**
Weaver, John, 18, 25
Weidman, Charles, 133
Weisberg, Shari
	posters by, **99**
Weitzman, Martin
	poster attributed to, **60**
	posters by, **83, 107, 137**
Welch
	poster by, **148**
Welles, Orson, 56
	photo, **57**
West, Russell W.
	posters by, **39, 47, 51**
Weyhe Gallery, 21, 78
Whitley, Kenneth
	poster by, **103**
Woodcuts, 21, 22, 36, 76, 84, 96,
	116, 125, 127, 165
Workers Education Program, 87
Works Progress Administration
	photo of march, **29**
	photo of rally, **28**
World War II posters, 31, **142–151**
Wright, Richard, 138
Zigrosser, Carl, 21, 78